Effective Communication and Empathy

How to Communicate Better With Social Skills and Confidence to Create Lasting Relationships and Connect Effortlessly With Charm, Charisma, and Witty Banter

Richard Garraway

Table of Contents

YOUR FREE GIFT 6

Introduction 7

Chapter 1: The Necessity of Social Skills 10

Understanding Social Dynamics 10

Why Social Skills Are a Must 12

Essential Social Skills You Need 14

Deficits in Social Skills 17

Communication: A Crucial Aspect of Social Skills 20

The Impact of Technology on Social Skills 22

Emotional Quotient: The Foundation of Social Skills 24

Chapter 2: Social Discomfort and Social Anxiety 27

Social Discomfort Versus Social Anxiety 27

When Shyness Really Is Social Anxiety 29

Signs You Are Socially Awkward 31

ANTs and Social Anxiety 33

Techniques for Managing and Reducing Shyness 34

Ways to Overcome Social Anxiety 36

The Importance of Positive Self-Talk 38

Gradual Exposure Therapy for Overcoming Social Anxiety 39

Chapter 3: Effective Communication 41

What Is Effective Communication? 41

The Benefits of Effective Communication 42

Barriers to Effective Communication 43

Verbal and Non-Verbal Communication 46

Verbal Communication..46

Non-Verbal Communication.............................47

Written Communication Skills.............................49

The Importance of Active Listening......................50

Practicing Assertive Communication.....................52

Effective Communication in Virtual Settings..........54

Learning the Art of Persuasion............................56

Chapter 4: Developing Empathy............................58

The Importance of Empathy and Perspective Taking........58

Emotional and Cognitive Empathy........................60

Empathy in Building and Maintaining Relationships...........62

Barriers to Empathy..63

Tips for Cultivating Empathy.............................65

The Basics of Empathetic Communication..............67

Chapter 5: Building Social Skills.............................71

The Role of Self-Awareness in Developing Social Skills.....71

How to Improve Social Skills..............................74

Social Etiquette...77

The Importance of Social Etiquette......................78

Common Rules in Social Etiquette.......................79

Cultural Competence......................................81

How to Become Culturally Competent.................82

Developing Social Confidence............................84

Chapter 6: Effortless Connection...........................88

What Is Witty Banter?....................................88

Developing the Art of Witty Banter.....................89

Improve Your Confidence................................89

What Is Charisma? 94

How to Network Effectively 97

Creating Positive First Impressions 100

Chapter 7: Your Guide to Lasting Connections 103

The Importance of Healthy Relationships 103

The Role of Effective Communication in Relationships 105

Building Healthy Relationships 107

Ways to Achieve Conflict Resolution 109

The Role of Vulnerability in Building Healthy Relationships 111

Cultivating Mutual Respect in a Relationship.................112

Creating and Communicating Healthy Boundaries...........115

Practicing Forgiveness and Compassion 118

Navigating Changes in Relationships Over Time 120

Chapter 8: Personal Growth 123

Strategies for Enhancing Personal Growth........................123

Putting Yourself Out There..129

Prioritizing Self-Care...133

Conclusion 136

THANK YOU!..138

References..139

YOUR FREE GIFT

As a special thank you, I'm delighted to offer you a free gift to deepen your conversation skills.

Introducing " **The Ultimate Conversation Starter Kit:** A comprehensive guide with conversation topics, questions, and tips to help individuals start meaningful and engaging conversations with anyone."

To claim your free gift and embark on this life-changing journey, visit: https://richardgarrawaybooks.com/Free-Gift-1

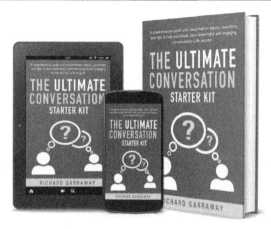

Inside this Starter Kit, you'll discover:

- A comprehensive collection of conversation starters and topics to confidently initiate meaningful discussions.
- Proven techniques to maintain a smooth conversation flow and keep engagements engaging and dynamic.
- Practical tips for overcoming social anxiety and navigating social settings with ease.
- Insightful guidance on nonverbal communication, active listening, and conversation etiquette to foster genuine connections.

Thank you for your support and trust in "Effective Communication and Empathy." Let's embark on this path together.

Richard Garraway

Introduction

Have you ever wondered about your communication skills? Do you think you are good or bad at it? We all have thought of these questions before. Why is it important to have effective communication skills? Our everyday lives are dependent on communication because we won't be able to live without interacting with other people. Nowadays, communication does not only take place in person, but also through the internet. Moreover, understanding effective communication is a skill we need to connect better with others and become successful in life.

Effective communication means understanding the points we wish to convey and making the audience understand them. Our personal and professional life both depend heavily on communication. It means that learning the particular skills that will enable us to exchange information with others with better understanding and clarity.

There are various benefits as to why we must learn how to communicate effectively. What are these advantages? Effective communication brings people closer and fosters better relationships. It also develops trust building when there is a misunderstanding between the parties involved and inspires people to develop their creativity so that they can accomplish more. In the workplace setting, it is beneficial to strengthen a person's sense of accountability to improve their work performance. Most importantly, effective communication helps us communicate our messages and aids in creating a connection with our audience.

We have seen that there are many benefits of effective communication. Do you wish to unlock your highest potential, accomplish your deepest desires, and socialize better with people? Then, you have come to the right place to delve into effective communication. This book provides you with insights on how to communicate better in your daily life. First, you will learn how important it is to have good social skills for you and the people around you. Afterward, it will help you understand what social anxiety is and how to overcome them in a healthy way. Then, it will offer you tips on how to socialize effortlessly by developing empathy, cultivating communication skills, and understanding the art of witty banter, charm, and charisma. Furthermore, you will be given step-by-step instructions on how to build and maintain your relationships and make them last through effective communication skills.

You might be wondering why you should be listening to me right now. Well, I love helping people overcome issues with their social interactions, especially on how to build long-lasting relationships. For the last five years, I have been researching the best methods for connecting with other people easily and steering clear of social anxiety. My goal is to assist you to become free from communication challenges since what you are about to learn has helped me conquer my own struggles with these issues, as well as improve my ability in connecting with the people around me. Having had firsthand experience with different communication challenges throughout my life, I am certain and confident that the ideas I provide in this book will be extremely helpful to you.

This book will assist you in mastering how things work in effective communication and learning the essential information that is relevant and practical to you. After reading this book, you will realize how easy it is to connect with others since the communication skills you learn will come naturally to you. This is your time to begin learning about effective communication and you will feel ready the next time you come across a person with whom you want to connect.

Are you ready to build your confidence and maintain lasting relationships with your loved ones through effective communication? Let's start this journey.

Chapter 1: The Necessity of Social Skills

Understanding Social Dynamics

It is crucial for us to take social dynamics into account as the world keeps evolving and the technology era expands. This part of communication is frequently overlooked because most people only focus on abilities like speaking or writing. It is widely believed that communication skills are only related to how we speak, read, or write, but we also need them in order to learn about social dynamics. This ability involves knowing how people think and interact with those around them. Communication is basically only an aspect of social dynamics, but social dynamics encompasses every part of human interaction. Understanding these concepts is crucial for effective communication because it helps us better comprehend who we are and those around us.

Social dynamics refers to the behavior of a person that comes from their interactions with other people, such as in friendships, family, romantic relationships, corporations, and so on (Oberhagemann, 2020). A person's behavior, how it affects them, and how others see them are the main focus of this dynamic. This means that social dynamics point to the process by which individuals develop into more educated and responsible people who have a good life in a society free from the influence of selfishness or resentment.

We can better understand social interactions by observing and examining them. By doing so, we can understand ourselves and other people in social settings. It makes no difference whether we participate in the interaction personally or simply observe it because we can still learn from them. In order to speed up the process of understanding social dynamics, we can also get information, knowledge, and practice advice from other sources.

Let's take a look at an example. A person's behavior varies depending on the people or groups they come into contact with. We will behave in distinct ways when we interact with our boss, parents, or children. There are interactions that require major shifts, but more subtle and minor changes also occur depending on the situation. This behavior is attributed to wearing a mask in some cultures. We put on a different disguise for each interaction.

Our actions, mindset, and communication style have an impact on social dynamics whether we are interacting with others in a group, in public, or at work. When we understand how to carry ourselves around people, we can be successful at influencing others and become successful in life.

Why Social Skills Are a Must

We all have heard about how crucial it is to learn social skills. When we do not fully comprehend social skills and how we can improve on them, it might be challenging to get better at them. Let's start with what social skills mean. Social skills are ways of communicating with other people that can help us succeed in social settings (Sander & Watkins, 2022). Every day, people communicate with one another in many different ways, including verbally, nonverbally, in writing, and visually. We use social skills every time we communicate with someone else. We may develop and sustain successful relationships in our personal and professional lives with the aid of strong social skills.

The following are crucial factors to keep in mind when discussing social skills. Learning social skills is possible because they are not always a talent we are born with. Since they are similar to all other skills, they can be learned and mastered through practice. We can pick up new social skills we are interested in and learn how to be good at them. In addition, social rules are also adaptable. They are often just considered to be guidelines. The better we are at socializing, the more we can go beyond these rules. This indicates that we should not always follow the example set by others because they might face different situations than ours. Instead, we need to respond based on what situations we are facing.

Social skills are a must since they may help us develop, sustain, and strengthen connections with our friends, family members, and coworkers. Establishing productive relationships requires strong social skills. These skills enable us to fully understand the feelings and needs of the people around us. Our ability to interact with people more effectively can help us establish strong and reliable relationships in the long run.

Furthermore, the key to social skills is good communication. Those who have good social skills can interpret another person's body language and comprehend the key points of a conversation better. Additionally, they have the ability to establish trust, thus making it simpler for people to be open with them.

When we have better social skills, we will also be able to establish and maintain friendships with others. As a result, we will feel happier and more fulfilled in life. With social skills, we can build trust and have so many different friends. The people in these relationships can be there for us when times are tough and help us when we require emotional support. Additionally, social skills also can help us avoid loneliness. Fostering social skills will give us the courage to approach those close to us when we are feeling lonely or isolated.

Excellent social skills are also associated with increased employment opportunities (Herrity, 2023). When we know how to socialize with people and carry ourselves around them, we will have better career advancement at our workplace. Having social skills gives us the chance to learn from and share information with people from other fields or industries. We can also assist our coworkers in challenging circumstances which will broaden our network to discover and seize new opportunities. When in a team, we can encourage others to complete tasks and achieve a common goal. If people trust us in the company, we may also share our expertise and mentor younger people. Those who are successful at their job will feel more motivated to be productive and perform better at work.

Essential Social Skills You Need

We are all aware that social skills are among the most crucial to have in order to communicate effectively. Human beings are frequently judged on their ability to communicate, which significantly affects a person's well-being. When someone is good at communicating with others, they will have a higher chance to become successful in whatever they do. However, when a person has no idea how to socialize or communicate, they might choose to isolate themselves in their room and feel like a failure. This is why we need to master social skills for our success and well-being. The following are some of the essential skills that we must consider learning:

Anger Management

When someone doesn't know how to communicate well, they might become aggressive and raise conflict during a conversation. Those who do not know how to manage their anger may also resort to violence. They may fight, shame, and criticize others if there are any opposing opinions. This will slowly erode everybody's self-esteem if they were to interact with them. The first thing to learn when managing our anger is understanding that violence is never acceptable, regardless of how furious we feel. There are many methods for handling anger. If we get angry at someone for what they did, we should never shout, call them names, or put our hands on them.

The following thing to do is to establish some clear boundaries with the people around us so that everybody is aware of what is unacceptable regarding aggressiveness or violence. For example, at home, you can establish a rule prohibiting serious discussions after drinking if someone you live with becomes violent when intoxicated. No one ever acquires social skills in one day, especially if they were not trained as children. However, anger management can be mastered as long as you practice it often.

Active Listening

If we wish to be better at communication, we need to master active listening. When listening to someone, we should hear and process the information first so that we can understand them well. We should focus on what they say rather than preparing a response before fully understanding all the points being made. However, there are times when our ability to process information properly fails, which can cause us to misinterpret their message. This is when active listening is needed and we can also ask questions when something is confusing.

For instance, you ask your partner to go on a date night and they decline your invitation. Instead of being upset because they refuse to go out, you ask them why they chose not to go out.

Then, after hearing their explanation, you give them their space to take a rest overnight.

Non-verbal Communication

One of the primary forms of communication is non-verbal. It includes interacting with others by using body language, like eye contact, facial expressions, tone of voice, and gestures. Even if we subconsciously utilize it in our daily lives, we need to pay attention to how we do it so that we may improve our ability to communicate with others. Furthermore, the information expressed verbally can also be improved even more through nonverbal communication. For example, you go to your teacher's office to ask for extra credit, but they look at the clock and show hesitation on their face. Instead of pestering and forcing them to listen to you, you get the cue and tell them that you can talk another time.

Conflict Management

Conflicts happen frequently in our lives. The likelihood of conflict is highest when there are two or more parties involved. Effective conflict resolution is one of the most crucial social skills that we need to learn. It is very difficult to resolve conflicts. Many people refuse to admit that they are wrong and frequently maintain their views on a problem, making conflict resolution increasingly challenging. We will need patience if we want to settle an issue with someone like this. Although the answer seems clear, it is vital to remember that the issue could not be resolved straight away. Even when there is an obvious solution, jumping to conclusions too quickly might make people feel excluded from making the decision. Conflict resolution involves recognizing the issue at hand and making an effort to resolve it without the use of emotion, but rather logical reasoning.

Self-Awareness

Self-awareness is the capacity to concentrate on ourselves and determine whether or not our behaviors, ideas, or emotions are consistent with our internal standards (Betz, 2022). If we have self-awareness, we can regulate our feelings better, match our actions with our beliefs, and accurately assess how other people see us. This enables us to be more conscious of how we speak to other people and become aware of their reactions as to what they are trying to communicate with us. Being self-aware is crucial for us because it helps us evaluate our progress and effectiveness in our personal and professional lives, and alters our course of action as needed. For example, when you become self-aware, you might realize that your tone of voice and facial expressions are sending the wrong impressions to others. Thus, you try to improve them instead of letting people keep misunderstanding you.

Deficits in Social Skills

Individuals with poor social skills frequently suffer more from anxiety, loneliness, and stress, which can have a detrimental effect on health (Blue, 2017). Having problems with social skills is not the same as being social. Someone might want to talk and socialize with others, but it does not work well when they try. They may find it difficult to strike up a conversation, appear strange, or act in a way that makes others uncomfortable. Some people might have a hard time reading social cues and complying with social norms. This can make it difficult for them to socialize, establish friendships, and collaborate with other individuals. Because of this, they might prefer to keep to themselves and be alone.

There are many causes for why some people struggle with social skills. What are these causes? Poor social skills are most frequently caused by a lack of experience. This happens when a person rarely socializes or talks to people. These days, it's normal for us to stay inside our rooms and avoid socializing with our friends and other people when we do not need to. Humans develop their skills by practicing them and experience is crucial in social interactions because of this. In actuality, those who have excellent social skills always claim that they simply chatted with many people and their past experiences built their skills. If we do not put ourselves out there and talk to people, we might even forget how to socialize.

Another cause of poor social skills is trauma. Past trauma can cause people to have negative feelings toward social interactions. Many people lose their social skills after facing a traumatic experience. For example, a cheerful child who used to like talking might become reserved after being bullied at school. Or when your parents refuse to appreciate your hard work at school, it upsets you so much and you choose to close yourself off from them.

Anxiety is also a significant issue for those who have poor social skills. When someone experiences a lot of anxiety, they tend to feel uncomfortable conversing with others. Even if a person has outstanding social skills, anxiety can produce uncomfortable circumstances since it makes it difficult for them to be confident. Additionally, anxious people typically struggle with communicating their ideas, which makes conversation difficult at times. This is why a lot of them choose to not socialize so that they do not have to feel anxious.

How can you tell if you have poor social skills? If you frequently find yourself in uncomfortable situations when speaking with others, you may have poor social skills. You may also realize that many people you speak with unexpectedly have a reason not to be around you. Some individuals are very honest about what they think, but others are nice enough to keep quiet. In my opinion, it is better when someone is honest with you so that you can improve yourself. If somebody ever tells you about how bad your social skills are, you should not get offended. Instead, you need to ask them to elaborate more on what parts you have to develop. In the end, you can become close to this person and they can help you navigate social interactions better.

Communication: A Crucial Aspect of Social Skills

The foundation of every human interaction is communication. It is the way we interact with others, as well as how we hear and process what is being communicated to us. It is not just humans who go through this process. Other living creatures, like animals and plants, also have unique means of communicating within their species. Because of this system of knowledge-sharing, they are able to flourish and survive in their natural habitats.

At its most basic level, communication is the process of passing information from one location to another (Barot, 2022). It will take a very long time to master communication skills. Some say that practice makes perfect, which means that we need to put ourselves out there more to socialize with others. There are various types of communication, such as verbal communication through spoken words, nonverbal through body language and eye contact, and written through writing on a piece of paper; and humans frequently combine some of these approaches to communicate with each other.

What Is the Importance of Strong Communication Skills?

Our personal and professional lives can benefit from improving our communication skills. A crucial life skill that should not be undervalued is the capacity to communicate information effectively and clearly. No matter how old you are, you still have time to practice communication skills. By doing this, we can increase our quality of life.

In our personal lives, excellent communication abilities can help develop and sustain our interpersonal relationships by facilitating mutual understanding. We know that every relationship requires good communication in order to work out. Many marriages and relationships have failed as a result of a lack of communication. These relationships deteriorate because of so many misunderstandings that happen and nobody wants to listen to one another. Communication is not just about talking and sharing our thoughts, but it is also about listening to what the other person has to say. Furthermore, communication is also essential in interactions with other family members. We will need to communicate things with our parents or siblings about different things. If we do not know how to communicate well with them, our relationships will suffer and we might even lose contact.

In our professional lives, communications are even more necessary to have. It is almost inevitable that we must show strong communication abilities if we are seeking a new job or a promotion to a better position at our workplace. During a job interview, we need to show the interviewer that we have proper body language and eye contact. We should also keep our focus during the interview process and answer the questions appropriately. We must demonstrate that we are prepared to work at the company. These can work the same if we are looking for a promotion. It is not enough to just be good at our jobs; we also have to learn how to advocate for ourselves to build trust.

These interactions can be made easier by having strong communication skills that enable us to convey our ideas while also listening to the other person.

The Impact of Technology on Social Skills

It is now very normal to see young people preoccupied with their technological devices and unaware of their surroundings. Many of them do not know how to talk to others properly in real life because they mostly communicate with their phones. Social skills are being lost in the younger generation as a result of the internet, which connects us to the digital world.

In this digital era, technology causes us to have fewer human interactions. People are starting to depend more on technology to connect with their family, friends, and coworkers instead of meeting them in person. During the Covid-19 lockdown, people needed to work from home so they only communicated with each other through the internet. Even after the lockdown was lifted, many still preferred to work from home instead of going to their office. Some might think that remote working is a great idea because they do not have to commute to work. However, it also had a negative impact on our social interactions. This means that people do not need to socialize anymore because of their online jobs. Also, more people begin to feel lonely because they rarely interact with others. When we do not communicate face-to-face for a long time, our social skills might become unavailable when we need them again.

Nowadays, most teens prefer to text instead of having real-life conversations with their friends. In order to be good at conversations, someone needs to know how to listen, ask questions, and understand the other person's body language. Teens in this era lack these skills, which means that they have no idea how to converse properly when they need to talk with someone in person. People who try to talk to them think that they do not care for the conversation because of their constant need to look at their phones. Face-to-face interactions involve the exchange of information through verbal and non-verbal cues that are set for the occasion (Fodeman, 2020). When teens refuse to look at the person they are talking to, they cannot process the information correctly and might misinterpret the message.

Kids these days also have very short attention spans. A short attention span is defined as the length of time we can maintain focus on something, such as work or listening (Hall, 2023). When a person is not paying attention and is bored during a conversation, it can be quite obvious. Those who have good social skills will know how to concentrate on what the other person has to say. We may find it difficult to concentrate on conversations if we have a short attention span or are prone to distractions.

The fact is that technology has significantly changed how we communicate with one another. It is true that nowadays we can interact with people across the globe, but it also worsens our social skills. What can you do to prevent this? You need to limit your screen time as much as you can and try to socialize with people outside when you have the opportunity.

Emotional Quotient: The Foundation of Social Skills

Emotional Quotient or EQ, also known as emotional intelligence, is the capacity to recognize, utilize, and regulate our own emotions in order to reduce stress, communicate clearly, connect with others, conquer obstacles, and solve problems (Segal et al., 2023). Those who have a higher emotional intelligence are typically more successful and happier at home, work, and school.

By being emotionally intelligent, we can avoid circumstances where we might act impulsively rather than logically. We can achieve more accomplishments in our lives by knowing how to manage our emotions and understand the feelings of the people around us. Having emotional intelligence can help us when we are in the middle of unpleasant discussions but do not want to offend anyone. It also assists us in keeping our emotions under control when we are feeling anxious or nervous. Moreover, it may also help in maintaining better relationships with our loved ones.

Emotional intelligence mainly consists of four characteristics (Segal et al., 2023; Ferry, 2023; Birt, 2023):

- **Self-awareness:** Having self-awareness means that we have the capacity to recognize our feelings, as well as how they influence our actions and overall mood. This helps us gain a more objective view of our abilities by identifying what we are good and bad at.

- **Self-management:** This means that we can regulate our emotions in an effective manner, take responsibility, keep our word, and adjust to changing situations. With self-management, we can also manage impulsive emotions when they appear instead of drowning in them.

- **Relationship management:** It is crucial to know how to manage our relationships with others when a crisis hits. When we are good at relationship management, we have the ability to effectively express our ideas, persuade others through how we speak and act, and collaborate well with them.

- **Social awareness:** When we have social awareness, we can empathize with others better. We also have the ability to identify other people's emotions, understand their worries and needs, and feel at ease in social situations.

Many of us often think that the only thing that matters is our IQ, but this is not true. Our EQ is just as important because no matter how smart we are, we can never be as successful as those who are good at communicating. This is the time for us to take action and learn how to better our emotional intelligence because it is the foundation of good social skills.

Chapter 2: Social Discomfort and Social Anxiety

Social Discomfort Versus Social Anxiety

Social discomfort is also called social awkwardness. We experience social discomfort when we feel uneasy and like a misfit in social settings. As humans, we survive by socializing with each other. However, not everyone has the natural ability to communicate well with others. All of us have felt uncomfortable or awkward when interacting with others; and if we can do it consistently, we can become better at communicating. There are no standards for diagnosis or even a clear definition for social awkwardness because it is more of a feeling, hence it is not a mental health condition (Raypole, 2019).

It might be uncomfortable for many people to be in social situations, particularly when they have to meet new people. Many of us have experienced a situation where we are afraid of saying the wrong thing, or even overthink that we cannot control the words that come out of our mouths. It is also not unusual for uncomfortable silences and awkward laughter to happen as well, and some people feel embarrassed if they are the ones who cause them. For some, social situations can be draining and it may be worse when they have social

27

awkwardness. Some of these people even try to avoid socializing as much as they can so that they can save their energy.

Being socially awkward isn't always a bad thing. However, it may become an issue if it causes emotional distress when hearing rude comments from others, always feeling like a misfit in social settings, and having a hard time connecting with people to make new friends. It can be very difficult to face all these issues, but we do not have to change ourselves. What we can do is learn how to be more comfortable in social settings and remove ourselves from a distressing situation so that it doesn't get out of hand.

So, does that mean social discomfort and social anxiety are the same? The fact is that they are different even though they share some similar characteristics. As I have explained the definition of social discomfort, let's now talk about social anxiety.

Social anxiety disorder (SAD) is a form of anxiety condition that makes people feel uneasy or afraid in interacting or socializing with others (Higuera, 2022). Those who suffer from this condition make it difficult for them to interact socially, make new friends, and participate in social events. They might worry that they will be watched or judged by other people. These people know that sometimes they do not have a reason to feel anxious or scared in social settings, but they feel helpless because they have no idea how to get over them. Moreover, social anxiety can be a consistent issue for some people; they often have a hard time performing their daily activities. These people can even struggle when they need to go shopping, talk to people they meet, or even eat at a restaurant.

When Shyness Really Is Social Anxiety

Many people suffer from social anxiety and it is true this can cause people to struggle, which can lower their quality of life because they are unable to do normal activities. However, some people also struggle to speak in public because they are shy. Those who have a hard time in social settings might think that they are just shy and do not have social anxiety. So, do you really have a social anxiety disorder, or are you just shy?

Just like social discomfort, shyness shares similar traits with social anxiety as well. Shyness is actually not as bad as social anxiety. Shyness often only manifests itself at particular moments; in unfamiliar settings, someone might feel shy in the beginning, but they can get used to their surroundings and start feeling more comfortable. Social anxiety is a bit different because a person might feel anxious or stressed out about a social situation they need to attend long before they experience it. It also doesn't just go away like shyness because it may persist throughout the interaction or even after it has ended.

Shyness also does not need to be treated like social anxiety. Usually, shyness does not get worse over time as long as we try to put ourselves out there and become more comfortable in new social settings. However, social anxiety can get worse if we refuse to address or treat it. In the long run, our ability to learn, succeed in our work, maintain financial stability, and maintain close relationships with our loved ones can all be severely harmed by social anxiety disorder (Cuncic, 2022a).

Social anxiety can also make people suffer from depression because they feel as though they have no choice other than to isolate themselves rather than interact with others (Abraham, 2020). This mental health issue can also make someone nervous before speaking in public. For example, if someone struggles with social anxiety and has to prepare for a presentation in class, they will overthink what will happen days before. The problem is that this overthinking process can cause them to lose sleep because their mind is always thinking about the things that could go wrong. Their heart might also race and they may shake or sweat often. Even after the presentation, they may worry about what others thought about their presentation and how people may have judged them.

After reading the explanation above, do you still think that you are just shy? Perhaps you might have a bigger problem, like social anxiety. It's better to contact a medical professional so that you can get diagnosed properly and get the help you need.

Signs You Are Socially Awkward

Those who are socially awkward are frequently unaware of this fact. The people around them also have no idea how to tell them in a way that does not hurt their feelings. Do you feel like people don't enjoy being around you? This is why you need to understand social cues so that you can be more approachable to people. The thing is, it might be challenging for people to disregard social awkwardness, regardless of how much they like you. The following are some of the signs that show if you are socially awkward so that you can work to improve them:

- **You struggle to carry on conversations:** When you are with your friends, it is hard to keep talking to them for a long time. You might realize that your conversations with them only last for a few seconds or minutes. Meanwhile, these friends are able to talk to each other for a long time. This can happen because you do not know how to make small talk. When someone asks you a question, you may prefer to keep your answer short without asking new questions and continue on with the conversation. You might also have trouble to keep talking when the other person stops. This can be very awkward when there are too many pauses.

- **You experience anxiety in social situations:** Social awkwardness may happen when someone has anxiety and fear when interacting with others. You may fear how others will perceive you so you spend your time thinking about what to say so that you do not make any

31

mistakes. After you talk, you might even overthink whether your words offended others or not. You choose to focus on the negative things instead of thinking that others might find you and what you spoke about interesting. As a result, you have difficulty having open conversations.

- **People avoid making eye contact with you:** Socially awkward people make others uneasy. Because they are not aware of their awkwardness, they might sometimes make strange comments and only focus on themselves during the interaction. When they do this, others start to feel uncomfortable and decide to alienate them. When someone is constantly avoiding eye contact, you need to be aware of the cue and improve how you carry yourself.

- **You always lead the conversations because the other person looks bored:** When someone looks bored while talking to you, it might mean that they want to stop the conversation. You can even pay attention to their body language if they want to leave or want you to stop talking. You may see that they look away or keep watching the time. If you often experience these situations, you need to look into yourself and see what you can change.

ANTs and Social Anxiety

Automatic negative thoughts, or ANTs, are thoughts that might arise as a reaction to our everyday situations, consciously or subconsciously (Cuncic, 2020). These negative thoughts are often unfounded and can worsen social anxiety. We all have thought negatively about ourselves and our situations before, but these thoughts can affect those with social anxiety in a bad way. Negative thoughts come and go; most of the time, we can just ignore them. However, if we have social anxiety, these thoughts can stay in our minds for a long time. For instance, before giving a speech, you might think that you are stupid and people will ridicule you because of it. These thoughts can fill your mind, which will affect your actions and behavior.

Negative feelings are experienced by everybody. They are inescapable and we should not try to avoid them. However, we should not allow these thoughts to bring on new problems in our lives. For this reason, it is crucial to work on becoming conscious of and controlling our automatic negative thoughts. We can manage how we feel by challenging and refocusing our way of thinking.

How do you identify these negative thoughts? We need to start by recognizing uneasy emotions as they appear. Paying attention to our feelings will help us identify when we are having unpleasant automatic thoughts. For example, you realize that you feel nervous and sad. By knowing these emotions, you will have the chance to figure out why you are feeling them. After that, we need to see the source of these feelings. Perhaps you will see that these emotions come from your thoughts. Then, we can identify a pattern.

We frequently develop unfavorable patterns as a result of negative automatic thoughts. These negative thoughts will keep appearing and strengthen the impression we already have. For instance, negative automatic thoughts always come up after you have a fight with your partner. Lastly, we need to see if these thoughts make sense. If someone else experiences the same thing, would they feel negative emotions? Do you think these thoughts are irrational? Once you can identify your automatic negative thoughts, you can find ways to stop them from appearing or manage how you respond to them.

Techniques for Managing and Reducing Shyness

There are many reasons for a person to be shy, such as never being taught how to socialize by your parents or having low self-esteem. Despite the reasons that make us shy, we can develop the confidence to establish relationships with people and understand ourselves more in the process. How do you overcome shyness? Here are some techniques you can consider:

- **Start small:** Starting big is impossible because it might not work out and become very overwhelming for us to handle. If you are not good at speaking in front of people, you shouldn't start by giving a speech to a big audience. You need to set achievable goals that you can manage step-by-step. These goals can make you comfortable, slowly but surely. Perhaps you may start making conversations with your coworkers or friends. Since you are already comfortable with them, it will be good practice before moving to talking to strangers.

- **Explore your strengths:** Shyness is not bad if it does not get in your way. However, if it hinders your success in life, you need to take action. Shyness needs to be overcome if it causes you to miss out on opportunities. Sometimes, shyness can keep you in your comfort zone instead of using your strengths. This is when you need to go beyond and explore your abilities more. When you know you are good at something, your confidence level will improve and you can overcome your insecurities.

- **Stop sabotaging yourself:** There are times when you become your own enemy. You have to be mindful when you talk to yourself and try to overcome shyness. You must convince yourself that you deserve what you have and are good at things. Try to ignore negative thoughts that come to your mind to overcome shyness.

- **Accept failures:** We cannot always accomplish everything we want. There are times when we have to face setbacks, but this is not the end. Just because you fail at one social interaction, it does not mean that you cannot try again. Getting comfortable with socializing takes time and you must not feel disappointed after only one failure. No one is perfect so you should not give up because your journey is still long.

Ways to Overcome Social Anxiety

It's not the end of the world if you suffer from social anxiety. There are many ways you can overcome and minimize it. You need to look for methods that will work for you through practice and experimentation. It is important to note that social anxiety requires time to overcome. There is no instant fix out there. What you can do is develop coping mechanisms and learn how to deal with the discomfort it causes. Once you find your own ways to handle it, you can better control it when it comes back. The following are several techniques for overcoming anxiety:

- **You can start by facing negative thoughts head-on.** There may be instances when you feel unable to change how you feel or think. The fact is that it is possible to reduce your social anxiety by facing and challenging them rather than overlooking or drowning in them. For example, you have to attend a social event and negative thoughts start to fill your mind. You need to start by identifying these thoughts and considering why you have them. These scenarios in your head have not happened yet, why do you have to worry about them? They might not occur in the future because there are chances that things may go differently than you think they will. Shift negative thoughts into positive ones and convince your mind that everything will be okay.

- **You need to improve your lifestyle.** Because the mind and body are intertwined, how you care for your body can have a big influence on how you feel about yourself and how anxious you are. You do not have to start big in order to feel more confident and better manage your anxiety feelings. You can begin by integrating exercise into your daily life. If you never work out, your body will not feel good and you get tired easily, which can cause negative thoughts. Start by taking walks around your neighborhood or going to the gym. When your body is healthier, you will be more positive in socializing with others.

- **You should socialize and engage with others more.** You can seek out social events that can benefit you in overcoming your anxiety. Perhaps you can begin by reaching out to the community, religious institution, or joining an event. You can also look for charity groups in your area and ask them if you can contribute. Before going out, you need to practice so that you do not get confused. In these social settings, try to make friends and ask them to teach you how to socialize better. Things can be difficult at first, but once you get to know more people, it will be easier.

- **You need to be kind to yourself during the process.** The struggle to overcome social anxiety is real. There will be instances when you have negative thoughts and revert to old patterns. You might even feel more anxious after putting yourself out there more. However, it does not mean that you have failed and should stop trying. When this happens, you need to relax and take a moment to arrange new strategies and try again.

The Importance of Positive Self-Talk

A person's inner conversation that helps them feel better about themselves is known as positive self-talk (Richards, 2022). Typically, people use positive self-talk as a way to convince themselves that everything will be fine when facing difficulties. They do this to motivate themselves so that they can keep going even when things get tough. For example, you have just gotten rejected for a job application. Instead of dwelling on negative thoughts that you are a failure, you positively talk to yourself that there are other companies out there that will hire you. You know that you have what it takes and a great position is waiting for you.

A study on positive self-talk indicated that students who read a self-affirming remark before giving a speech or presentation felt less anxious and nervous than those who did not (Shadinger et al., 2019). Speaking in public often causes people to feel anxious and uneasy. If we do not know how to be positive and assume the worst will happen, we cannot present our points effectively. If we have a low confidence level, we might also indulge in negative self-talk, which will affect our communication skills in a bad way.

How do you improve your positive self-talk? The most important thing to do is to recognize negative feelings when they come out. Perhaps your mind says, "I can never do it, this is impossible." You need to shift this statement into, "I can handle and finish this without worry." You can even write your negative and positive thoughts down and compare them. Once you see them on paper, you will see which ones are better and make a decision. If you struggle with negative self-talk, this is the time to better yourself by practicing positive self-talk.

Gradual Exposure Therapy for Overcoming Social Anxiety

Exposure therapy is frequently employed to assist those suffering from anxiety disorders and it makes someone confront their fears in a secure space while being guided by a skilled therapist. In this therapy, someone who has anxiety disorders is faced with situations, events, or objects that can trigger their fears (Herndon, 2021). As time goes by, their anxiety reduces and becomes more manageable.

A skilled therapist can determine the origin of our social anxieties, their level of severity, and whether they have prevented us from engaging in activities we would otherwise enjoy. There are different ways that a therapist might use exposure therapy. One of them is real-life confrontation. For example, if a person has anxiety about speaking in front of a crowd, the therapist might suggest talking in front of a much smaller group of people. Another way is to ask the person to imagine a situation that they are afraid of and try to challenge it.

Exposure therapy needs to be done slowly without rushing. Over time, the person can tolerate the things that trigger them better until they can get over it. However, if the person is exposed to these triggers too fast, they might be discouraged to try it again and stop the therapy altogether. In order for it to be effective, the person needs to do it step-by-step and accomplish small goals along the way.

Chapter 3: Effective Communication

What Is Effective Communication?

The process of transferring or delivering knowledge or information from one person to another through a chosen method or medium with a clear goal in mind is referred to as effective communication (Naz, 2023). Effective communication requires at least two people who can both articulate their ideas properly and comprehend the topic or goal of the discussion while letting everyone involved to communicate their perspectives. It can be used for people to share their needs, understand the responsibilities assigned to them, and interact with others around them.

Communication itself can take many different forms because humans can communicate in a variety of ways. As previously stated, the forms of communication are verbal, non-verbal, written, and visual. Additionally, communication can occur face-to-face, through phone calls, or via social media. Everyone has their own level of effective communication and it can influence their personal and professional lives. The more effective your communication is, the better you will be in regard to your work and personal aspects. Also, we can examine how good we are at communicating in our work.

41

The Benefits of Effective Communication

Effective communication is a valuable skill that we must learn, especially if we are trying to advance in our professional lives. Do you want to know the advantages of learning how to communicate effectively? The following are some of them:

- **Effective communication gives us a better understanding:** Developing strong communication skills will help us show that we comprehend what the other person has to say. For example, you will have to communicate with your superior or colleague in the workplace. When you can effectively communicate about a project, it means that all of you will be more productive and the project can go smoothly from the start because there is no place for confusion.

- **Helps us resolve problems:** If we have an issue about something, we will need to know how to express it in words. For example, you do not like something that your partner does. Through effective communication, you will share this concern with them rather than bottling it up. After that, you can resolve the problem together without fighting in the process. Or perhaps you have an issue with your coworkers and you tell them about it instead of gossiping. By doing this, you can create an honest work environment.

- **Establishing trust with others:** For example, someone decides to criticize you. Rather than getting offended and angry about it, you try to reflect on it. Afterward, you may ask that person to elaborate on what aspects you could change. Through effective communication, people will respect you more because you do not get swayed by emotions, even being criticized. As a result, they will feel more comfortable around you, which leads to more trust and respect.

- **Conflict can be avoided with effective communication:** When problems arise, it is very easy to get frustrated and blame others. However, this leads to more conflict and issues. For example, when an error happens in a project, you need to assess where the problem lies and avoid pointing fingers. By doing this, you and your coworkers can get past these challenges more quickly and move forward with projects as a whole.

Barriers to Effective Communication

There are numerous causes for communication to go wrong. The message may not always be understood exactly how we intended. The truth is that there are barriers that may present throughout the information exchange. When barriers alter our intended message, it may cause doubts and misunderstandings in the process. This is why we need to learn about these barriers so that we can find solutions when facing them later on.

For communication to be effective, we need to have trust and be honest with each other. Any kind of communication becomes quite challenging when these things do not exist. For instance, if you do not trust your partner because they have cheated on you in the past, you probably will never believe anything they say, even though they are telling the truth. Or perhaps if your coworkers suspect you are withholding information, they will feel tense and assume the worst. When you attempt to communicate with them, it will be harder for them to understand your perspectives.

The second barrier is the lack of listening skills. Effective communication relies heavily on listening to the other person. When talking to someone, we need to listen and process the information so that we can respond accordingly. However, if we refuse to listen, there will be confusion that arises and we might assume things that are not true. It means that we will not get to other people's needs because we are not listening to them.

Language and cultural differences can also become barriers to communication. It is critical to comprehend how communication differs between cultures. When we have a conversation with someone, we need to pay attention to their cultural background to avoid misunderstanding. If we fail to understand cultural differences, we run the danger of insulting the other person. For example, the same word can mean different things in different languages. If we do not understand this distinction, they could be offended.

In the workplace, a communication barrier can happen when someone is dissatisfied and has a lack of interest in their work. When someone does not like their job, they will not put in the effort to do their best. In other words, they are not giving it their all. This might make other people frustrated because they don't collaborate well. This barrier is possibly the most challenging to get past unless the person decided to quit or alter their mindset about the job.

Sometimes conflict may arise for other reasons. When it happens, the people involved will have a hard time communicating with each other. Conflict may cause resentment; and when people do not like each other, they can never talk without assuming the worst about one another. When a problem is not resolved, it tends to escalate. Before beginning an important conversation, it is better to solve the conflict first.

The last barrier is a physical obstacle. It is true that we can communicate through the internet nowadays. However, it does not work as well as when you talk to someone in person. For example, there are many people who work remotely these days. While it is good that they do not have to commute to work, it is often difficult to get information when they only have emails or calls to rely on as means of communication.

Verbal and Non-Verbal Communication

We already know that communication is an important skill that we have to master. However, did you know that communication does not only happen through words? Communicating through words is called verbal communication, and communicating with your body language is known as non-verbal communication. Let's see more of their differences:

Verbal Communication

Verbal communication refers to the exchange of information with others through words in speeches or writing (Surbhi, 2018). Words are used in verbal communication between at least two people to exchange information. The effectiveness of this communication method can differ because people have their own levels of skills. This relies on the words you choose, tone, speech clarity, and voice volume. We will know how effective we are at verbal communication by seeing how people respond to us and the feedback we get from others.

To be better at effective communication, we need to think about the people who are listening to us. This means that we have to pay attention to the audience and modify our words or messages accordingly. Verbal communication is very easy to control because we can control what we say or write if we feel that it becomes ineffective. What we need to do is communicate what we want to say and if the audience misinterprets our messages, we can try to correct them.

Effective communication relies on both the speaker and the audience. Although we have no influence over the audience, we can make an effort to convey our message with better clarity. It is easy for misunderstandings to happen, so we need to learn communication skills if we want to avoid them.

Non-Verbal Communication

Non-verbal communication was explained a little bit in chapter 1. Let's explore it further. Non-verbal communication is a method that takes place without the use of words; and while it can support spoken words, it may also be in direct opposition to them (Surbhi, 2023). This communication method is crucial because it reveals critical details about the situation, such as how somebody may be feeling, how they process information, and how we can interact with others. We can benefit from mastering the art of non-verbal communication in our personal and professional lives. There are some essential non-verbal communication types that we can learn. Let's explore them:

- **Body language:** This refers to how a person poses their body in response to a conversation, their surroundings, and their feelings (Keiling, 2023). It is also something that is very clear to see and understand. It might reveal a lot about our feelings for someone and vice versa. For instance, when someone is anxious or irritated, they may cross their arms. Or you can conclude that they are not very interested in the discussion. When someone talks to you with their arms on the side, it means that they are engaged in the conversation and willing to listen.

- **Eye contact:** This is another aspect of communication because it can show respect for the other person. Eye contact shows that we are interested in the discussion and paying attention to the message. When someone often looks away or focuses on their phones, they might be bored or want to get out of the conversation. They might also show disrespect for the person speaking.

- **Facial expressions:** This type of non-verbal communication is very crucial to learn. We can show that we are engaged through our expressions. Perhaps we can move our mouths or brows to show how we feel in a situation. For example, if someone is shocked about something, they will open their mouth wide and raise their eyebrows.

Written Communication Skills

In this modern era, the ability to write effectively is essential. In contrast to verbal communication, it involves written words instead of spoken words. Written communication allows us to intentionally pick and tweak our words before delivering them. In a professional setting, the majority of jobs require us to know how to write emails, texts, and documents. When we can write effectively, we can clearly communicate the message and avoid misinterpretation. Nowadays, most companies and schools rely on written communication for their operation and information sharing. How do we write better? Let's see some steps for this:

- **Identifying a goal:** Every written communication has its own goals. Before writing an email or message, you need to clearly find the goal. Our writing will be clearer if we have a specific goal. No matter what our goal is, we need to figure it out as quickly as possible.

- **Writing our point clearly:** Because we have time to choose our words carefully, we need to pay attention to them. We need to write concisely, even though we might think this is our moment to enchant the readers with poetic language and emotional statements. When we write clearly, our readers will understand what we have to say better and formulate any questions they may have about it.

- **Proofreading and checking for grammar mistakes:** Developing this ability is crucial, particularly if we are writing in a professional setting. Checking for grammar and spelling is a skill that can be perfected with practice. Once we have gone through this process several times, we can write better.

- **Using the right tone:** This aspect is very important in the workplace. In a professional setting, we need to write formally. Typically, we can write informally with people we are close with, but we should avoid doing this with a client or supervisor.

The Importance of Active Listening

We often listen passively when we hear anything, relying on our brains to recall them later on. But effective communication relies on active listening to work out well. Learning to listen actively well takes effort and patience. Once we are good at this, we can improve our relationships and connect with new people.

Active listening means being involved in the communication process. In order to effectively communicate, we must be able to listen to the other person's words while also attempting to understand their meaning and purpose. This means that we also need to give our undivided attention when someone is talking.

When we listen actively, we show interest in the other person and participate enthusiastically in the discussion.

This is an essential communication skill because it promotes honesty and transparency. By demonstrating that we are listening to the other person, we foster trust and give them the impression that what they say is important. Active listening also helps us reduce misunderstandings, make it easier to resolve disagreements, address issues, and create a more encouraging environment for collaboration, whether at home or our workplace. This is very different from passive listening in which we are not engaged at all in the conversation.

How do you become better at active listening? Here are some techniques to follow:

- **Maintaining eye contact:** Eye contact is an essential part of active listening. This shows the other person that we are focused and engaged during the discussion. Additionally, it demonstrates that you are not being sidetracked by anything else and you have their full attention.

- **Asking questions:** When the other person pauses, we can ask questions for clarification. This lets them know that we are listening and try to process their message. This will also help us get more understanding when we are confused about something. We will show interest and eagerness to learn more.

- **Keeping judgment to ourselves:** A good listener will refrain from offering unwanted advice, suggestions, or comments. We also need to avoid talking over the other person, even if we disagree with their opinions. Sometimes, someone does not need our opinions because they just want to be heard and we can talk if they ask us to.

- **Being patient:** We need to be patient when listening to someone speaking. Let them talk without interruption. We should not bring up stories about ourselves if the conversation is about the other person. If we want to give our opinions, let them finish and ask for permission to talk.

Practicing Assertive Communication

Assertive communication includes being honest about our wants, needs, and feelings. It is a communication skill that can help us manage ourselves better. We may use it to lead others in a better direction and make them listen to what we have to say. It is the capacity to confidently and clearly communicate our thoughts. Those who are good at assertive communication have better self-control and care about the opinions of others.

Let's take a look at an example. You are about to go on a vacation, but you still have some tasks you have not finished.

Then, you ask an employee to take over and help you. They say that they cannot take over everything because they are already busy with their own workload. Instead of getting angry, you choose to only give them half of your tasks and delegate the rest to another person. When you do this, that employee will respect you more because you care about their situation and are not forcing them to do everything.

Being assertive means that we know how to balance ourselves. We need to be open and honest about what we need while also thinking about other people's needs. Assertive people are confident and know what they want, but they present their arguments clearly, openly, and empathetically. This skill also can help us better our mental health and well-being in the long run (Raypole, 2020). How can we become more assertive?

- **Valuing ourselves:** Before we can be assertive, we need to start understanding ourselves. We need to believe in ourselves and our values to other people. Self-belief will lead to self-confidence. When we are confident, it is easier to be assertive. By doing this, we also realize that we deserve to be respected.

- **Expressing our needs with confidence:** If we wish to reach our full potential, we need to ensure that our needs are met. This is why we need to express our needs with confidence so that others know what to do. We should never wait for people to get us what we want. We have to take the initiative and make plans to reach our goals.

- **Being open to feedback and criticism:** We need to be humble and positive when receiving feedback and criticism. If we get criticism, we should not get irritated or angry at the other person. We have to look within and reflect on what is being said. If you want, you may also ask the other person to explain their criticism and how you can improve yourself.

- **Learning to say no:** Assertive people know how to say no because they are not people-pleasers. If we often say yes to something we do not want to do, we need to learn how to decline them. For instance, if a colleague asks you to do their job, but you are busy, you can say no in a polite and respectful way.

Effective Communication in Virtual Settings

We can stay in touch and communicate effectively by interacting through video platforms like Zoom or Google Meet. However, as we join more online meetings and spend more time every day looking at our computer screens, we must ensure that our virtual communications are meaningful, interesting, and effective. How do you better communicate in a virtual setting?

- **Avoiding distractions:** During a virtual meeting, it is easy for us to find excuses to zone out or get

54

sidetracked. This is when we need to reflect within ourselves and take notes of what can be helpful in this situation. By doing this, we can teach our minds to become aware of when they get distracted and to concentrate on the current situation. In a virtual meeting, we can practice noticing when our minds stray away from the present, identify the distraction there, and then refocus.

- **Understanding online etiquette:** We all have by this point either personally encountered or observed the consequences of bad online etiquette. Having a little fun or acting more casually than normal occasionally in a meeting is not necessarily a bad thing. It is true that in a virtual meeting, we do not have to wear a full suit or makeup anymore. However, there is new etiquette to follow in virtual communications such as turning off our cameras or muting our audio and using in-room discussions appropriately.

- **Joining on time:** When we arrive late at a meeting, it will show that we do not find it important. If we have a virtual meeting, we need to join early, like 15 minutes before it starts. When we fail to stay on schedule, this means that we have no respect for others. This will also send a bad message to our reputation.

- **Choosing our words wisely:** In virtual meetings, the words we use and the tone we project can occasionally sway people's thoughts in our favor or against us. This is why we need to be careful how we choose our words and stay away from any that discriminate against others.

Learning the Art of Persuasion

We have learned that information exchange is the foundation of effective communication. This involves developing strong relationships with others, paying attention to their message, and attending to their needs or issues. However, there are occasions when the direction of a discussion must be specific, such as when we must persuade people to understand our point of view; persuasion can help us with a situation like this. Have you met someone who is so persuasive that they can be convinced easily? Can you also learn all those skills? Of course, we all can do it.

However, before we learn how to be more persuasive, we need to understand that persuasion is not the same as manipulation. Being manipulative means that we force someone else to believe what we say or coerce them to do something they do not want while persuasion involves influencing others to do something that can be advantageous for us both (Nazar, 2013). Then, how do you become better at persuasion? Here are some tips:

- **Identifying the audience's interests:** We can modify how we act and behave to suit the audience's interests when communicating with them. For instance, we need to speak in a soothing tone to shy people to make them more comfortable when talking to us.

- **Not being pushy:** It has been explained that persuasion is not manipulation. This means that we cannot push or coerce people to believe our ideas. When we are being pushy, people might get defensive and refuse to listen to what we have to say. Rather, we need to show confidence and an honest attitude, which will make others trust us.

- **Complimenting the other person:** People are happy when they get complimented because it makes them feel good. When we compliment someone, they will feel at ease around us, making them trust us more. In this situation, it will be easier to persuade them.

- **Focusing on the point:** No one likes it if we keep circling around the topic without getting to the point. People will get bored when we do this. Instead of giving long and difficult explanations, we should make it more simple.

Chapter 4: Developing Empathy

The Importance of Empathy and Perspective Taking

Empathy is the ability to comprehend what somebody else thinks, feels, and experiences, which is one of the best persuasion methods (Marotta, 2017). This involves knowing and understanding others' viewpoints and what leads them to have these perspectives. Practically every area of our lives benefits from empathy. It enables us to connect to the people around us and influence the world in a positive way. Moreover, empathy also lets us have compassion for people.

In a personal setting, empathy is necessary to establish better relationships. Relationships require nurturing, care, attention, focus, and compassion. Without empathy, all of our personal relationships would eventually fall apart. If we only care about our own things in a relationship, the other person will be hurt. For instance, if one partner in a romantic relationship refuses to consider the other's point of view, there will probably be so many problems that arise. Everyone has their own unique experiences, which means that no one will think exactly the same. In a relationship, each individual brings their unique perspectives, hardships, and ideals. This means that it is crucial to understand our partners' thoughts or they will feel neglected, which will make the relationship suffer.

In a professional setting, empathy is important to connect with our coworkers and make our work go smoothly. Our workplace can work well if we have teamwork. This means that we have to get to know our team members to work well with them. For instance, if you work together with others on a project, you need to understand their perspectives. Without empathy, getting into arguments and conflicts is much simpler. Or if you are a leader, you need to pay attention to the emotions of your team. If you cannot understand how to motivate them, your team's performance will also suffer. When a team member makes a mistake, you should get angry or shout at them. You need to hear their explanation and ask them to do better next time. Trust can also be built through empathy because people will feel comfortable with you when you pay attention to their perspectives.

Empathy is also beneficial for the world and society. Empathy is crucial, particularly because it results in compassion. It is easy to stay in our comfort zone when we do not have to suffer, but helping people will show us that not everyone can be as comfortable as us. When a disaster happens, empathy will make people relate to the victims. This encourages them to take action and jump in to provide assistance where they can. Humans are willing to help others in need because they are aware that if the situation shifted in their direction, they too would require support. When we have compassion for each other, the world becomes a better place. With empathy, we can support those in need when we know that we have more to give.

Emotional and Cognitive Empathy

Empathy is typically only thought of as the ability to understand another person's perspectives. But studies have revealed that there are other varieties of empathy; the main categories are emotional empathy which is experiencing another person's feelings and cognitive empathy which is understanding how others think and feel (Clarke, 2023). When discussing empathy, we need to understand these two categories so that we can learn it better.

Emotional Empathy

When we have emotional empathy, we actually experience the emotions that another person is feeling; the emotions we experience will feel like we are in the same situation as the other person (Clarke, 2023). This occurs if we have gone through similar experiences and we understand why they react that way. For instance, if your friend is sad and depressed after getting cheated on by their boyfriend, you may know exactly what their emotions are because your ex did the same thing to you.

This type of empathy can be good or bad for us. Emotional empathy is beneficial because it allows us to easily comprehend and experience the feelings of others. This is important in a friendship; when we can relate to our friends' experiences, we can help them and establish better connections. It can also be good for medical workers; the ability to take care of patients effectively is essential and when they can respond appropriately to a patient's feelings, they will be better at doing their jobs. Additionally, emotional empathy can assist us in helping people in distress.

Emotional empathy is not good for those who feel overwhelmed easily. When we experience others' emotions, we might get overcome by them and find ourselves powerless to respond to the situation. Even though we can experience another person's feelings, we should not take them too personally because we may not be able to control them. If we find ourselves in these situations, we need to take a step back so that we can provide assistance for the other person. For medical workers, it can cause burnout and so if you are one, you need to learn how to control your emotions better and avoid dwelling too much on another person's situation.

Cognitive Empathy

Cognitive empathy, also called perspective-taking, means that we know how another person thinks and feels (Eatough, 2023). This involves analyzing the circumstance to learn how the person behaves because specific behaviors are related to various emotions. Cognitive empathy lets us assess the behaviors of others and respond accordingly, which means that we can modify our actions and words when interacting with them. For instance, if you see your friend is having emotional discomfort, you will pay attention to what they have experienced recently and find the best course of action to comfort them.

Cognitive empathy is a skill that can be learned and people understand it as they experience life. When we communicate and interact with others, we will understand them better as we go along. Once we become better at this, we will know when someone feels distressed or angry and why they feel that way. Even though we do not feel like we experience the same emotions as the person like in emotional empathy, cognitive empathy helps us to relate to them. With it, we can comfort or calm others when they need our support. We will not overlook their emotions even if we do not feel the same way. This will lead to better relationships with those who come in contact with us.

Empathy in Building and Maintaining Relationships

Empathy is a strong force that we can use to build and maintain our relationships with others. It is an important tool to establish trust and intimacy so that we can feel like we belong around people. This also makes us take more action when someone is having a hard time and help them go through their situation. With empathy, we are willing to understand and value people without asking them to change who they are and we accept people for how they are. It also helps us become more loving, compassionate, and non-judgmental. We do not feel the need to control and judge people because acceptance is the key here.

When we are dissatisfied in a relationship, we tend to blame another person for it. Without empathy, we would force the other person to change themselves instead of looking within ourselves. There are many ways that we attempt to influence others to change who they are; we would judge, criticize, punish, withdraw ourselves from them, etc. What we need to know is that we cannot change others if they are not willing to. This will only lead to the destruction of the relationship.

Empathy here helps us reflect on our actions and communicate the problems in the relationships. When a conflict happens in a relationship, we should not try to win the argument because it is not a competition. When discussing the topic, it is also important to listen and process our partners' perspectives and share ours in a respectful way. Once we have discovered the issue, we can together solve it. After that, we can all grow and learn to be better in the future. It can be difficult at first to learn to be more empathetic when we do not want to be wrong. However, we need to understand that a relationship will never work without empathy because we cannot understand or communicate with each other well.

Barriers to Empathy

Our lives need empathy to go smoothly, without it, we can never communicate or interact well with people. However, learning empathy can be difficult at times. In fact, various barriers may arise that prevent us from being better at empathy skills. What are these barriers? Let's explore them:

- **Fear:** This barrier can affect the way we socialize with people and also influences our willingness in showing empathy. When someone has low self-esteem or confidence, they will feel that they are not good enough at anything, which means that they will be scared to express their empathy. We should never run away from problems and rather use empathy to connect better with people. Our inaction can make others suffer, especially in a personal relationship.

- **Personal boundaries:** Many of us have past trauma and when we see someone in a similar situation, we feel the need to step back from them. Ideally, we can communicate these boundaries so that we can still show empathy, but it can be very difficult. For instance, you lost your parents in an accident and your friend likes to complain about their parents to you. You might not want to become a support system for them because you do not have any parents and the tragedy still traumatizes you. This is okay as long as you communicate these feelings to your friend. Both of you need to understand each other because you still need to heal yourself. If you have a good friend, they will understand your boundaries.

- **Stress:** When we feel stressed, we cannot think rationally. We might focus on ourselves and our situations and ignore the people around us. Perhaps your parents have shouted at you when they feel stressed. This does not mean that they do not love you. In that situation, they might not be thinking straight, they feel overwhelmed, and their stress clouds their minds.

- **Selfishness:** In this modern world, we all have busy lives. We feel like we do not have time to care for others. We already have our families, jobs, schools, etc. We are too preoccupied with these things and we choose not to care for those in need. For example, your neighbor just got into an accident. Instead of visiting them and asking how they were doing, you chose to ignore them and focus on your already busy life.

Tips for Cultivating Empathy

We have learned how important empathy is for our personal and professional lives. I know that not all of us know how to be empathetic sometimes. However, empathy is a skill that can be learned with practice. Are you interested in becoming more empathetic? The following are some tips for cultivating empathy:

- **Talking to new people:** It is frequently useless to try to imagine what someone else is feeling. To understand people, we can strike up a conversation with strangers or ask our friends or coworkers to lunch to talk to them. We should ask them questions such as how they are doing and how their day is going. We can also follow individuals on social media who come from diverse racial, religious, or political views. In our daily lives, we need to set aside our phones when talking to people so that we can understand how they act and behave in order to show empathy to them.

- **Joining hands with our communities:** We can join the communities around us and go to events to meet different people. Working on a project with others will improve our personal skills while also helping us connect. When we have better connections, we will eliminate the differences that could divide us from each other. For example, you can join a charity event, a church community, a support group, or a political event.

- **Listening and sharing with others:** It is true that we need to listen to others to understand how they feel. However, we have to also show that we are humans. Establishing a strong and compassionate relationship requires having confidence in them to hear and understand our true feelings and thoughts. Empathy is not only about understanding people but also about letting them understand us.

- **Concentrating on our similarities:** We all have our own prejudices and biases toward others. Sometimes, we might even assume the worst about people according to stereotypes. When we treat others in this way, we cannot appreciate our differences and think that we have no similarities at all. Instead, we have to focus on our similarities and understand that differences do not matter.

- **Using our imagination and being creative:** Oftentimes, many of us frequently believe that someone does not deserve empathy because they are different from us. This is why we need to use our imagination when showing empathy is difficult to do. We can show empathy to everyone, even in impossible situations or to the people we hate.

The Basics of Empathetic Communication

In communication, empathy is an important aspect to have. When we can empathize with the other person, we will pay attention to what their message is and not only focus on what we want to say. However, communication with empathy is never easy and this is why we need to know the basics of empathetic communication.

Knowing How to Listen

When we have empathy for someone, we will listen to their message and perspective so that we can understand them better. Try paying close attention the next time you are speaking with someone. This does not only mean keeping your mouth closed when the other person is talking but also preventing your thoughts from straying away. Many times, we become preoccupied with our own thoughts and forget to pay attention to the other person. Listening encourages us to become involved in what people are passionate about.

We need to continue to hold back after the other person has finished talking. We have to start with processing the conversation and then ask questions about things that are not clear. By doing this, we can make sure that we understand the message and show that we respect them and care about what they say. The next time we talk, the other will probably show the same respect for us as well.

Recognizing Other People's Communication Styles

In any environment, people have different personalities that make them have different communication styles. There are people who are extroverts who are easy to talk to and those who are introverts who prefer to stay silent and keep to themselves. When talking to someone, we need to observe and understand their communication styles. Thus, we can adjust the way we talk accordingly. By doing this, we will improve our communication skills and people become more comfortable being around us.

In a professional setting, you will see that extroverts tend to dominate conversations while introverts let them talk over them. If you ever find yourself in these situations, you need to ask the extroverts to pause and give others a chance to speak. You may also encourage introverts to speak more and express their thoughts in a respectful way.

Identifying Your Own Communication Style

Another essential thing to do is to identify our communication style. It can be challenging to evaluate ourselves accurately, so this is why we need to ask others to assess our communication style. We can tell the other person that we are trying to improve our communication skills and that we value their honesty. After they have given us some insight into our communication style, we should classify it into our strengths and shortcomings. This will assist us in identifying our areas of improvement and the skills we need to learn to be better.

For example, in a romantic relationship, you can ask your partner to give you some feedback. Perhaps you often interrupt your partner in a conversation. Maybe you yell at your partner sometimes. After knowing these facts, you can thank your partner and take action to fix the communication issues.

Controlling Your Emotions and Paying Attention to Others' Feelings

Before a challenging conversation, we need to prepare ourselves. First, we can make a list of important things that we would like to discuss. Before we provide a solution, we need to offer the other person some time to take in the information. We should provide them with the time and space to think properly.

If we see that the other person is not in a good mood, we need to reschedule the discussion for another time. If they look upset or frustrated during the conversation, we need to pause, let them think, and continue when they look more relaxed. Being empathetic means that we care about others' feelings, so we should never force someone else to be in a difficult conversation.

Chapter 5: Building Social Skills

The Role of Self-Awareness in Developing Social Skills

Chapter one talked about self-awareness a little bit. It has been explained that self-awareness means understanding our personalities, ideas, feelings, and behaviors. Self-awareness leads us to better grasp how we influence others, how they see us, and how to control the way we feel and behave. We have learned that social skills are very important in our personal and professional lives. Self-awareness is an essential skill to have if we want to improve other social skills. What are some advantages of having self-awareness?

- It helps us recognize our emotions and control them when interacting with others, which means that we can make people feel important in a discussion.

- It allows us to feel more at ease with ourselves so that we can interact with others in a true and caring way.

- It prevents us from talking over people and lets them finish with what they want to say before responding.

- It helps us communicate with people more deeply since they feel respected and comfortable with us.

- It assists in establishing stronger relationships with others because we know how they perceive us and how to change these perceptions in our favor.

- It improves our ability to collaborate and work with others.

There are many benefits to having self-awareness. This means that we need to do our best to learn this skill. What can we do to build our own self-awareness? Let's take a look at some tips:

- **Being open-minded:** When we have control over our emotions, we can be more attentive to other people's feelings as well. To be better at socializing with people, we need to understand them and what they can give us. For example, you are a leader who knows your team members' feelings and what they offer you. You will let them do their job and work well with them. You will also realize that you do not always have to be the best or do everything by yourself when you open opportunities for your team.

- **Identifying our strengths and shortcomings:** Those who are self-aware know what they are good and bad at. Even if they have shortcomings, they can still thrive in this space. Knowing these things will help us decide whether we need assistance or not in a difficult situation. We cannot always be good at everything, so if our shortcomings make us stuck, we need to seek help from others.

- **Setting boundaries:** We need to set boundaries with the people around us. We should be kind but also say no when necessary. We cannot always say yes to people because they might end up taking advantage of us. Self-awareness helps us realize our value, which means that it is important to set boundaries so that we do not get disrespected.

- **Thinking about how our actions impact people:** We frequently act without thinking things through. Many of us are selfish and only care about our own desires and needs. It is true that self-awareness allows us to understand our emotions, but this is not the only thing; we have to understand how our actions and emotions impact others. We can get through challenging circumstances by being more thoughtful of people.

- **Saying sorry when we make a mistake:** We are not perfect and we can make mistakes sometimes and that is perfectly okay. Self-awareness teaches us to look into ourselves when we make one and apologize for it. Perhaps you forgot your marriage anniversary because of work or you yelled at your partner during an argument. When these instances happen, you must say sorry so that everyone can move forward.

- **Learning our emotional triggers:** Self-aware people are able to recognize their feelings while they are arising

73

and unfolding. Rather than suppressing or denying our feelings, we need to deal with them before speaking with others. If we do not understand our emotional triggers, we might lash out at people even though they have done nothing wrong.

How to Improve Social Skills

Developing our social skills can be beneficial to us in different aspects of life. Social skills are crucial since they can improve our communication skills. Because of this, we can develop, sustain, and create better relationships with the people around us. The following are some ways to improve our social skills.

Doing Things in Person

Nowadays, it is very easy to get stuck in our rooms without meeting other people at all. There are many apps to use for everything such as for food, groceries, or household items. This means that we do not even have to step outside of our houses to get everything we need. Most people can even get their entertainment at home by watching Netflix or YouTube all the time. I know that these online services usually offer so many benefits and can save us money and time. However, they keep us disconnected from the outside world. Our social skills will deteriorate if we do not interact with people frequently.

This is why we need to do things in person instead of getting cooped up in our rooms all the time. For example, you can shop for groceries at the supermarket instead of online shopping. This way you can talk to people you meet at the grocery store. Or you can ask your partner or family to eat at a restaurant rather than delivery so that you may talk and ask how they are doing. The point here is to socialize more and there are many activities that you can do to interact with people to improve social skills.

Being Informed of the Current News

In order to have conversation starters, we need to stay updated with the current news around the world. We all have our own smartphones nowadays, and we can go to news websites or Youtube videos on what is happening around us. However, we need to stay away from negative topics such as religious issues or political problems that can create misunderstandings. We have to be polite and friendly when striking up a conversation with new people. To build a good relationship, we need to be respectful of others and their backgrounds. This is why we should never start a conversation about a controversial topic.

Putting Your Phone Away

These days, people do not talk to each other and focus on their phones all the time. It is even worse in public, no one talks to one another anymore. Before phones and the internet existed, we were essentially forced to interact and talk with those around us. Of course, there were books to read, but it was not as bad as today's technology devices.

However, nowadays it seems like everybody is buried in their smartphones. Additionally, using our phones to avoid engaging with people is seen to be something normal. We must put our phones away if we wish to interact and socialize with others. In the beginning, it will feel strange and possibly uncomfortable. However, if we want to start talking to people, we must first indicate that we are available to speak. Placing our phones aside will tell people around us that we can be approached for a conversation. We may also look around to find others who are available to talk with.

Starting Off Small

It can be difficult to start big whenever we want to improve a skill. Just like any other skills, social skills need to be started in small ways first. We can begin small by communicating more with those we socialize with every day. For example, you often go out to eat at a restaurant, and if the waitress asks about your day, you can respond and ask another question back rather than only answering with a single word. Though the waitress is a stranger, you have interacted with them before, so you will feel more comfortable making small talk. Or you can contact a distant family member that you do not talk to often.

Focusing on the Situation and Getting Out of Your Head

Many people become preoccupied with thinking about their next words to the point where they neglect paying attention and taking part in the discussion. It is very difficult to fix if it has turned into a habit. However, we can learn to watch out for it. When we have a discussion with someone else, we should pay attention to our minds; do we care more about what we need to say next or what the other person is saying? We might be shocked by how frequently it occurs.

In most cases, only being conscious of this tendency will help us improve. However, if we still have trouble after some time, we can try meditation. We can do meditation for around 10 to 15 minutes a day. Through meditation, we can learn to focus on the current moment and help our minds from straying away when in a conversation.

Social Etiquette

The use of proper social behavior, often known as etiquette, helps us advance in life by establishing stronger relationships (Sethi, 2021). Social etiquette makes us reliable and trustworthy members of society by acting formally and appropriately in front of other people. The standards of social etiquette will keep changing, therefore learning them requires some time and practice.

Human beings are social creatures, which means that we need to interact and socialize with others to survive. In order to establish relationships, we must abide by certain social norms and rules. We need to follow social etiquette so that we can be polite and respectful around other people. Social etiquette not only lessens conflict and builds relationships, but it also shapes how other people see us. When we follow social etiquette, we can impress others. This will make them trust us more, which means that they will treat us with respect.

The Importance of Social Etiquette

Some of us might think that social etiquette only consists of pointless rules; however, we still need to follow them because it will be beneficial for us and others. The following are some reasons why we have to follow social etiquette:

- **It teaches us how to behave appropriately:** We need to behave differently in certain situations. When we learn good social etiquette, we can put it into practice even in situations we have never faced before. It is like a useful guide to show us how to behave in social situations.

- **It helps us interact more easily:** When people follow social etiquette in social interactions, they will not have to face unneeded misunderstandings and stress. This means that interacting with each other becomes easier. Additionally, it may decrease conflict that might result from these misunderstandings.

- **It makes us approachable:** The proper use of social etiquette will make us seem like caring people. When we are friendly and warm toward others, they will feel like they can approach us and that we are open to them.

- **It helps us create and sustain relationships:** When we are respectful and well-mannered, people trust us more. This means that people are drawn to us and we can establish stronger relationships.

- **It enhances communication:** How we behave around others is also a part of communication. Our social etiquette reveals more about who we are as people than the words we use.

Common Rules in Social Etiquette

Although social etiquette will change with time, there are some rules that can be applied in all settings in our daily lives. Let's take a look at some of these etiquette rules so that we can be better at interacting with others:

- **Having good manners:** No matter what social situation we are in, we need to always behave in an appropriate manner. Good manners include communicating with everyone with the utmost respect and politeness.

- **Being punctual:** We should never make others wait for us. We need to arrive on time no matter who we meet. This will show that we are professional and we respect other people's time. This will also leave a good impression on others, which means that we become trustworthy. For instance, if we have a meeting with a client at work, we need to arrive at least 10 or 15 minutes before the scheduled time.

- **Resisting the temptation to use our phones when talking to someone:** Everyone has a phone nowadays and it is difficult for them to stop looking at it. However, it is important to put our phones aside when we are in a conversation. This will show that we respect and hear what they need to say.

- **Covering our mouths when coughing or sneezing:** Nobody enjoys being sneezed on. Therefore, we need to cover our mouths when we feel the need to sneeze or cough in social situations, especially when we are eating or drinking with other people.

- **Holding the door for someone that comes after us:** Regardless of gender, we should never shut the door in the face of someone who comes behind us. We need to open the door until they can hold it. This will demonstrate your consideration for other people.

- **Saying thanks when someone does something for us:** If another person helps us or gives us something, we need to show our gratitude and say thanks to them. This will show them that we appreciate their nice gesture, which will make them happy as well.

- **Avoiding sensitive topics in public:** We should never make others uncomfortable around us. One thing to avoid is talking about sensitive subjects when in public. We need to talk about it when we are in private.

Cultural Competence

If we want to establish better relationships with others, we need to know how to engage and communicate well with people from other cultures who have different beliefs and backgrounds. Cultural competence is the communication skill that allows us to interact with those from different cultures through positive actions, attitudes, and behaviors (Riserbato, 2020). When we have cultural competence, we will be better at maintaining relationships. In a professional setting, it is essential to increase productivity because there will be less conflict among employees. Cultural competence teaches us how to respect everyone no matter what backgrounds they come from.

Here are some benefits we can get from having competence:

- **It gives us a better understanding of different perspectives:** Those who are culturally competent are frequently more likely to listen to and accept other people's opinions and viewpoints. They understand that people have different experiences in life and they are willing to accommodate others. This means that they become better at collaborating with people even though they have different beliefs.

- **It offers us more ideas:** When we can collaborate with people from various cultures, we will learn new ideas that we have never thought about before. People have their own way of thinking, so when a problem arises, it will be easier to find a solution because everyone can offer their opinions.

- **It helps us become better listeners:** In order to understand other cultures, we need to listen to what they are saying. This means that we have to actively listen and process the new information given to us so that we can know the ideas behind it. If we refuse to listen, we cannot become culturally competent or get along with people from other cultures.

- **It improves our empathy skills:** Being culturally competent means that we have to care about others, which will improve our empathy toward them. This means that when others have issues, we will be there to support them no matter what their backgrounds are.

How to Become Culturally Competent

The first step to being better at cultural competence is to keep an open mind. When we are open to others, it will show that we are ready to accept others and their differences. People have unique life experiences, so we need to be prepared when they end up having different ideas and beliefs than us. We need to be curious about others' cultures so that they become drawn to us. We need to try to understand their feelings and thoughts and be open to help anyone that comes in contact with us.

Making positive changes is another important thing to do. We need to go beyond our comfort zone to become culturally competent. If our beliefs and ideas are outdated, we can never interact with people from different cultures. We have to get rid of outdated perceptions and views that can hinder our journey to becoming culturally competent. We need to make changes in ourselves first before we can understand other people or our effort will be unsuccessful.

Furthermore, we have to be more sensitive to other people. In order to become culturally competent, we need to be sensitive to others about their experiences. The issue is that ignorance can occasionally lead to offensive remarks or actions that can cause conflict. This is why we need to understand other people's cultural traditions and backgrounds first before talking to them. We have to familiarize ourselves with them and refrain from making assumptions.

We need to also become adaptable and flexible. As we engage and interact with people globally, we need to remember that people from other cultures view the world in different ways. This is why we have to adapt ourselves to various cultures. We can begin by being aware of how unique every culture is. This stops us from projecting our own feelings or bias onto other people. We have to be curious and broaden our understanding of different cultures. This way, we can immerse ourselves in them and increase our sensitivity toward them.

Developing Social Confidence

When we are confident, it means that we have faith in our abilities and judgments (Morin, 2023). This means we have trust in ourselves to manage our lives or whatever situation we have to face. Some people say that confidence is our way to success. This is true because if we do not have confidence in doing something, we will never achieve it. In social settings, confidence is also an essential aspect. If we have no social confidence, we cannot communicate or interact with people at all. I understand that not all of us have high levels of confidence because some people are shy or have social anxiety. However, confidence is a skill that we can learn and it is never too late to do so. Would you like to learn and understand how to be more confident during social situations? Let's explore some methods to do this:

Preparing Your Social Interactions

If we do not feel confident enough in social settings, preparation can be a useful strategy to ease our nervousness. We can find out as much information as possible before the meeting and practice how we will behave and act in these situations. We can plan ahead what to do and what to expect so that we do not feel shocked when we arrive there.

For instance, someone invited you to a dinner party at a restaurant. You could ask them how many people would attend and if you knew them. If you recognized anyone from the guestlist, you could talk to them first before talking to strangers. Perhaps you could ask your friend about the name of the restaurant and look up the menu to choose what to order. Maybe you could choose what clothes to wear days before the dinner party to ease your anxiety. When you plan things ahead, you will feel more confident and in control of the situation.

Moving Outside of Your Comfort Zone

In order to gain social confidence, we need to put ourselves in circumstances that are completely outside of our comfort zone. For instance, you can make small talk with total strangers you meet at a coffee shop or on public transportation. We should not start with big steps, but begin small and increase it gradually. We can make the challenge more difficult each time. We may make a list of social circumstances that give us anxiety and sort them from easy to hard. Then, we should start overcoming them from the least challenging ones.

It is possible to be socially confident through practice. By doing this, we can get rid of our shyness and nervousness in social settings. It can be very draining at first because we are not used to it. However, we will feel more comfortable talking to people as long as we keep practicing it.

Concentrating More on Others

When someone does not have social confidence, they have a tendency to overthink their own actions. They are concerned with how other people perceive them and their behavior. When we do this, we will always feel uncomfortable because we assume the worst in social situations, particularly if we have to interact with strangers. This is why we have to shift the focus to others. We can observe what they do and say and learn interesting things about them. We can perceive others just like how others may perceive us. Moreover, we will become better listeners when we concentrate on others. This will then establish a better relationship for both of us. The other person may also become our friend or future partner as the relationship progresses.

Believing in Yourself

We need to be comfortable with ourselves first before we can be good at social interactions. We have to accept and believe in our authentic selves to feel more at ease in social situations. Self-belief leads to confidence; we must have faith in our abilities to overcome things. When people see that we believe in ourselves, they know that we are confident in interacting with them. As a result, they are more drawn to us and we can build better connections with them. Before we put ourselves out there, we need to understand ourselves through self-reflection by spending some time alone or journaling. When we know ourselves, we can show others who we are when interacting with them.

Learning From Your Mistakes

It is important to note that when learning something new, we cannot always be perfect and might make mistakes. In social settings, making a mistake can lead to awkwardness. However, we have to know how to take the lessons from the situation and apply them in the future. Most of the time, social mistakes do not have a significant long-term impact, so we should not feel bad when we make mistakes.

Let's say that you are meeting your coworkers for lunch. When talking to one of them, you forget that they have broken up with their partner and accidentally ask them about it. This situation makes you feel bad. If someone else makes this mistake to you, you probably won't mind and just let it go. All you need to do is apologize to your coworker for the mistake and move on. You should not overthink or dwell on it too much. What you have to do is to be careful when talking about someone's private life in future situations.

Chapter 6: Effortless Connection

What Is Witty Banter?

Witty banter is a fun and smart conversation method that can liven up our communication with others and help us establish connections much faster (Hailey, 2022). When we use witty banter, we can make our interactions with people more engaging and interesting. When we tease or joke with the other person, we can create trust and intimacy for each other. But witty banter must not be obnoxious, disrespectful, or patronizing. We need to draw a line between respectful teasing and blatantly making rude comments.

Only a few people have wit as a natural talent. It is a talent they are born with because, from the start, they are comfortable with themselves and the people around them. This natural ability helps them communicate that flows smoothly, toss in hilarious and funny comments, and get other people to laugh without trying too much. However, not all of us have this talent and we often struggle to be good at witty banter. When we do not have this natural skill, it can be challenging to improve without practice.

However, we also should never force ourselves to use witty banter when we are not good at it. Why? Because it might make people uncomfortable. We all must have interacted with somebody who was trying too hard to show that they are funny and smart, but they just came across as a little forced. In this situation, we would probably get secondhand embarrassment. This is why we should learn how to be better at witty banter instead of forcing or embarrassing ourselves in front of other people.

Developing the Art of Witty Banter

Because many of us are not born naturally with wit, we need to learn and practice to be better at it. Are you intrigued to learn how to be good at witty banter? Here are some ways you can do so:

Improve Your Confidence

We need to stop rambling and stumbling over our words in order to be witty and make funny comments during a conversation. This is why we have to improve our confidence and become comfortable in social situations. If we are uneasy around others, we can never be good at witty banter. This involves working on our speaking abilities so that we can feel more confident.

To practice this, we should not start with strangers but with the people who we are comfortable with. All we need to do is to make an effort and talk more when we meet our friends or family. When a funny thing appears in our minds, we can say it and watch how others react. It will not always work the first time we try. However, based on our observation, we can see what other people enjoy hearing. Through practice, we will gain a lot of confidence that we have never had before. One bad experience does not define who we are, because learning a new skill takes time and effort.

Tell Old Stories

The easiest method to improve our witty banter is to share stories that come naturally. We can do this by thinking about our own old stories or past experiences. Because we went through the experiences, we may add details that provide the story some dimension. After that, we can include witty and humorous comments that will make the storytelling more fun. Before we speak to someone, we can list some stories that we would like to tell. We can practice them at home prior to the conversation so that we can become more confident. Through practice, we will also sound and look more natural when telling our stories.

Make It Light-Hearted

Witty banter is typically humorous and light-hearted. We can use it to tease and make jokes around our family and friends. However, we should not go too far. We need to make comments that are funny but not offensive to others. This works best when we are just responding to what someone said. For instance, if a friend makes a comment on your makeup, you can respond with something like, "But I can date your dad with this look." You should not get offended and say rude comments in this situation. This might sound childish, but it is funny and can make others laugh. It also does not cause any harm to your friend. The important point here is to be fun and humorous without hurting the other person's feelings.

Ask Questions

To be witty in a conversation, we need to have enough material to talk about. This means that we have to ask the other person some questions and advance the conversation. We also should not only ask yes or no questions, but those that need longer responses to get to know the person. When they talk, we need to motivate them to speak more. To be better at witty banter, we have to allow the other to talk and then make the occasional witty remarks.

This means that we need to actively listen to them so that we can make witty comments according to the topics they talk about. We should not interrupt them and wait for the right moment to add our comments. It can be annoying for the other person if we keep making unwanted comments before they even say what they want.

Refrain From Making Fun of Others

When developing witty banter, we need to avoid making fun of other people. I know that we can connect with people who hate the same thing or person as us. However, we should not make fun of people to be witty. By doing this, we will appear cruel and mean instead of being funny. If we want to be better at witty banter, we need to avoid talking badly about others and focus on positive things instead. We will not enjoy it if somebody is gossiping about us, so we should avoid this at all costs.

Use Facial Expressions

To spice up the conversation, we can use our facial expressions in addition to witty remarks. When talking to someone, we can utilize a variety of facial expressions to make things more fun, such as a cheeky smile or a lip bite. Everyone has witnessed someone make a witty comment while simultaneously managing to maintain a perfectly straight face as if they are unaware of how hilarious they are. This may make others laugh more because of their unawareness.

Expand Your Knowledge About Various Cultures and Subjects

The key to being good at conversations is to learn new knowledge. Our ability to connect and engage in witty conversation with people will increase as we broaden our knowledge. If we keep doing the same things every day without gaining new insights, we will run out of conversation starters. We can do different things to gain new knowledge, such as checking international news, reading interesting books, joining a charity event, volunteering in a local community, and more. When our lives are boring, we will never be able to engage in exciting conversations.

Stay Focused on the Present

When we spend so much time thinking during an interaction with someone, we might become too nervous to make a witty remark. We should not think too much and focus on what the other person has to say. When we are dwelling on our thoughts, we will get distracted. This means that we will never have the opportunity to engage in witty banter. We need to make ourselves focused on the present and observe what is being said so that we can make witty comments properly. To practice this, we can take deep breaths and pay attention to our environment. Once we realize we are in our current situation, we can move our focus to the other person.

Dive in Without Hesitation

Many people are hesitant to be witty in public out of concern that they may offend someone with what they say. When we have the chance, we should try to show our wits. If we are capable of accomplishing something but are choosing to hold back out of fear, it is unfortunate for us because we can never learn. As long as we can keep everything fun and lighthearted, we have nothing to worry about. We should never be scared to engage in witty banter so that we can practice more.

Even if we end up making a mistake, it is a normal thing. Other people have probably experienced it too. As long as we do not do it on purpose, we will be okay. What we need to do is say sorry and carry on the conversation.

What Is Charisma?

Charisma refers to the energy you produce in others; it is the way you uplift, encourage, and affect them (Reid, 2020). When used effectively, charisma enables us to make others feel more energized and motivated after talking to us. This is an important talent to have, especially for those in leadership positions.

We all have met a charismatic person before. They know how to make us feel important and they stay in our minds even after we stop talking to them. We think of them as wonderful people and we would like to keep in touch with them. We feel energized and inspired just by talking to them. When they talk, we are drawn to listen to and focus on what they have to say. Moreover, we will feel good after spending time with them.

Charismatic people have a big influence on people and this is what makes them succeed in communication and relationship building. Would you also like to have an impact on people? Let's take a look at charismatic people's habits that you can follow easily:

- **Smiling more:** When we smile, it means that we will look more approachable and glad to be around others. By smiling more, we can be more charismatic, but we need to mean it. Smiling is not about pretending to be happy but about communicating that we are curious and interested. Even though it sounds weird, we can work on our smiles in front of the mirror. We need to make it look as natural as possible. With practice, we will feel more comfortable about smiling around others and showing our genuine smiles.

- **Pacing our speech:** When we are passionate or anxious about something, our speech patterns frequently change. This is why we need to practice pacing our speech and talk more consistently. No one likes it if we suddenly talk too fast or too slow. When we know how to pace our speech, we will look more assured about what we say and be in control of the situation. This will also radiate self-confidence.

- **Displaying a sincere interest:** When talking to someone, we need to show that we are interested in the things they talk about. We can do this through direct language and facial expressions. When we are involved and listening to them intently, the other person will typically feel appreciated and respected. However, when we get distracted, they will feel ignored, which will decrease their trust in us.

- **Noticing small details:** When in conversation, we need to try to remember the small details that they tell us. The next time we talk to them, we can mention these details so that they will feel important and respected. As a result, they will open themselves up because they trust us. These small details can also become great conversation starters.

- **Sharing about our passions:** When speaking with somebody that we are not close with, we can establish our confidence by talking about our passions. By doing this, we may step back from the situation and redirect our focus from the fact that we are talking to a stranger. It can be uncomfortable talking to a stranger, but when we learn how to be more charismatic, things will be easier with time.

- **Calming our nerves:** Being charismatic means that we need to be confident. However, it can be difficult if we get nervous easily in social situations. It is normal to get anxious when we have to talk in front of people. Before we talk to someone, we can practice our speech first. This will make us more comfortable as well. Another method to calm our nerves is to meditate; we can learn how to control our breathing and take time away from overthinking.

- **Being humble:** To become a charismatic person, we need to be humble around people. However, it does not mean that we have no self-worth. Being humble here involves respecting people's values and not thinking that we are more important than everyone else. It also means acknowledging others' successes without bringing ourselves down. We can look arrogant if we are not humble enough; however, we will also look weak if we are too humble. This is why we need to have the right balance of humility.

- **Choosing our words carefully:** Our choice of words will influence how people behave and act around us. We need to use positive words more than negative ones so that we can uplift and empower others. Everyone wants to be around people who are joyful, energetic, and motivated. Not only will our words impact the people around us, but they also work as positive self-talk to push us to be better.

- **Being vulnerable:** Even though charismatic people seem like they are not scared of anything, they are still vulnerable individuals. By being vulnerable around people, we show them our authentic selves. We need to accept our vulnerability so that others can see that we are open to them. People will be drawn to us because they see us for who we are. Perhaps we can try by telling our true opinions about a sensitive topic, but it does not need to be about our private lives.

How to Network Effectively

As professionals, we need to know how to expand our connections with people through networking. By doing this, we will meet and get to know people from various industries so that we can advance our careers. There are various ways to do networking nowadays, such as attending face-to-face and online networking events, joining seminars or workshops, and attending conferences. Whatever we choose to attend, there are some tips that we need to follow:

- **Before attending a networking event, we must set what we want to achieve there.** These goals need to be specific and clear. This way, our minds can focus on them without wandering or getting confused. For instance, you can say that your plan is to meet and talk with five executives from different companies. You may also set a goal to meet your favorite author and ask them about their new book. Perhaps you plan to look for new job opportunities by talking to people from the HR department. We can set any goal we want as long as they are reasonable so that we may stick to it.

- **We have to dress formally and professionally.** When attending a networking event, it is important to look organized and clean. This is why when choosing outfits, we must choose one that makes us look formal and professional. A first impression is essential in networking events because people will judge us based on how we look. Moreover, it is also crucial to choose an outfit that makes us comfortable so that we may stay confident throughout the event.

- **Pay attention to how we introduce ourselves.** Before we start a conversation with someone, we need to begin by introducing ourselves. When our introduction is effective and well, we can impress them and this may lead to a better conversation. With a good impression, we will also create new networks and connections with others at the event. We should prepare how we will introduce ourselves and rehearse it at home.

- **When someone is talking, we should listen actively.** Active listening is also a crucial skill to apply at a networking event. If we wish to build a new connection, we need to know how to converse with others well. By listening and processing what someone has to say, we can respond accordingly which might lead to a deeper conversation. We need to stop our minds from wandering in a conversation so that the other person does not feel ignored as well.

- **We need to be straightforward about what we want from the other person.** When talking to someone, we need to express our intentions in two to four sentences. If we talk too long without saying what we want, people will lose interest. Once they are hooked, we can then explain more about ourselves and what we do. It is also essential to use easy words that are easily understood. We need to avoid using slang words that not everyone understands.

- **If possible, we should take notes.** In a networking event, we will probably talk to so many people that makes it hard to keep up. When we find someone interesting, we need to take notes. Perhaps if we ask for their contact information, we can write it down in our notebooks. The purpose of networking is to establish future relationships and connections; when we take notes, we can keep in touch with people and follow up to better the connections.

- **We need to bring our business cards.** We should bring as many business cards as we can because we do not know how many people we will meet that day. We might meet hundreds of people that we can give our cards to. Exchanging numbers on our phones is possible, but it is not as fast as giving out a card. It is better to exchange business cards because they are more efficient.

Creating Positive First Impressions

First impressions are the conclusions we make the first time we meet a person and we establish this by observing their face, attitude, outfit, body language, and voice (Waters, 2021). I know that first impressions are not always accurate because we have not gotten to know the person yet. However, many people judge us based on their first impression of us. Our first impressions will stay in other people's minds for a long time and it will be difficult to change them. This is why we need to pay attention to how we want to impress people in our first meetings.

Let's see how we can create positive first impressions:

- **Attire:** When someone enters a room, people will first check out what they are wearing. How someone dresses will tell us about their attitude and personality. For example, in an office, you are probably not allowed to wear mini skirts. If you still decide to wear one, people will look at you weirdly and think that you are out of place. Their first impression will not be good because you cannot follow a simple dress code as a professional.

Before you dress up to go somewhere, you need to check what is allowed and what is not so that you do not embarrass yourself.

- **Eye contact:** When talking to someone for the first time, we need to make and keep eye contact. This will display that we respect them and pay attention to what they have to say. Before we start talking, we need to begin with eye contact and appropriately maintain it throughout the conversation. However, we should not stare at the other person because it will make them feel uncomfortable.

- **Punctuality:** To create a good impression, we need to always be on time. When we are late, we waste other people's time which means that we do not respect them. When the meeting is confirmed, we need to arrive at least 10 to 15 minutes before it begins. When we are the first to arrive, people will be impressed by our punctuality. This will show that we value others' time and we can serve as an example for them as well.

- **Honest and genuine:** When talking to people for the first time, we should be honest and genuine. We should not fake things and pretend like a know-it-all. No one likes someone who is being arrogant and likes to brag. When someone is speaking, we should listen and try not to interrupt. This way, we will show that we genuinely pay attention to what they are saying.

- **Smile:** When we smile, we will look like a kind and genuine person. We should smile sincerely so that people feel more comfortable with us. This will also show people that we welcome them and that we are open to listening to them. People can see if our smile is genuine or not; when we are being insincere, people will feel tense and offended.

- **Names:** In a professional meeting, we need to remember the other person's name. It can be difficult if we have to meet so many people at once, this is why we should prepare before the meeting takes place. We can write down their names and memorize them. If a person tells us their name, but it is hard to hear or difficult to say, we should ask them to spell it out.

Chapter 7: Your Guide to Lasting Connections

The Importance of Healthy Relationships

Human beings need to maintain relationships in order to survive. Relationships are important for our health whether physically or mentally. We also have a natural inclination to stay connected and get closer to the people around us. We might think that sometimes we can live just fine living without people, but being isolated from other humans will make our well-being suffer. A healthy relationship means that two or more people are able to empower and support each other when in need. It involves communicating effectively to minimize misunderstandings. When everything is communicated clearly, it will be easier to sustain a healthy relationship where everyone can be happy. The following are some of the advantages of maintaining a healthy relationship.

Having a healthy relationship helps us to act less selfishly. When we have no relationship, all we focus on is ourselves. Perhaps we only care about our well-being without worrying about others. However, when we have a relationship, we need to also think about other people. When someone needs us, we will go to them to comfort or help them. We become more caring about their feelings, not just ours. Caring about others' feelings is very important in establishing a stronger and healthy relationship, which will lead to a deeper level of connection.

We may also lower our stress levels. When we have a healthy relationship, we have someone else to support us in case we need them. For instance, if you are facing a hard time at work, you can tell your partner about it. You will have someone to listen to your rants. Perhaps when you experience a bad day, your friend can take you to a nightclub to dance your heart out. As a result, we will have less stress through the connections we have with other people. This is why we need to trust and turn to our loved ones when we experience any issues in life.

A healthy relationship assists us in learning more about ourselves. A relationship will surely help us to learn about other people, but we can also understand ourselves more. When we interact with others, we will see how we act and behave around them and how considerate we are toward them. Perhaps we think that we are not good people, but when we are in a relationship, we might see that we can do nice things for the people we love. This will definitely make us better people if we keep up with doing good things for others. However, it can also show us our negative behavior or actions. This will increase our self-awareness so that we can transform our way of life.

Additionally, we may expand our horizons. Establishing relationships means that we have to get to know the other person. This involves learning about their interests and passions. Perhaps we may find out about books or songs that we have never heard before. In a professional setting, we can also expand our network the more connections we have. We get to meet new people to talk and hang out with and understand their lives to be closer.

We will have someone that gets us. When we deepen our relationships, we will connect with our loved ones better. This means that if we have problems, we can turn to them without worrying about judgment. Perhaps we do not even have to tell them anything and they get our feelings and vice versa. Having a person we know on a deeper level is an amazing feeling, which is great for our well-being.

The Role of Effective Communication in Relationships

No relationship will become better if we do not know how to communicate effectively. A relationship can only work if the two parties can understand each other without too many misunderstandings. We all have heard that many relationships failed because nobody was willing to communicate and understand each other's needs. However, we would not want this to happen to us, right? This is the time we must step up and learn how to communicate effectively and apply it in our relationships.

It has been explained before that effective communication requires active listening to work. Listening to someone else when they are talking means that we show them respect. Even if we have a different perspective about what is being said, we listen because we care about the other person's ideas and thoughts. Effective communication in a relationship shows that we value and appreciate someone for being in our lives. In turn, they will also demonstrate how they care about us as well. When both parties have no idea how to actively listen, no message will be transmitted properly and there will be misunderstandings. The relationship will most likely fail because no one can find a middle ground for anything.

Effective communication makes us understand every perspective. The purpose of communication is to understand and be understood. It is not something we do to judge, invalidate, or fight. Even if we have disagreements, we need to be able to move forward by looking at different viewpoints. There must be a point where we can agree with each other if we try to communicate effectively. By doing this, we may also avoid getting into conflicts or fights. We can prevent unnecessary dramas and issues that may come up from misunderstandings. A key to this is to avoid jumping to conclusions before thoroughly listening and processing the message.

A relationship makes us more approachable. When we are in a healthy relationship, we need to show that our doors are always open. Effective communication leads people to believe that they can be comfortable talking with us. Perhaps a friend is facing a sensitive issue at home, when you offer them support and comfort, they will approach you to search for advice. Maybe we have heard of stories where married couples could not talk to each other about their issues because they were afraid of being judged. Even if someone is married, it does not mean that their relationship is healthy. To fix this, they need to be open with each other so that they can speak more comfortably.

Building Healthy Relationships

In a journey to establish a relationship, things will not go smoothly all the time. There will be ups and downs that we have to face. We are all imperfect humans and we can make mistakes, especially when we are in a relationship. We will struggle and suffer, but as long as we do it together, we will be able to get past it. We need to be willing to take the necessary actions so that we may create a healthy relationship. But how do we do this? Let's explore how we can bond with others more easily.

We are not scared of expressing disagreement. The key to a healthy relationship is when we can express ourselves freely without judgment. We should not be afraid to face a conflict. A relationship will suffer if no one is able to express their mind. This means that every emotion will be suppressed, which might explode in the worst way later on. A conflict once in a while is okay; this is important so that we can address the issues that have accumulated throughout the relationship. If we refuse to address a problem, it will get bigger and at some point, it might become the fall of the relationship. The point here is to solve conflict and disagreements without retaliation and humiliation from each party.

We need to understand that everyone makes mistakes. I have said that as humans, we are not perfect. This means that sometimes, people can make mistakes. If we wish to have a healthy relationship, we need to accept this fact and forgive others. If we truly care about someone, we have to forgive them when they apologize. Holding grudges in a relationship will be very toxic for the relationship and it might fail. We need to forgive and avoid holding grudges if we still want to maintain the relationship.

We must try to sustain an emotional connection with each other. Another important thing is to feel connected on an emotional level. We need to feel loved and fulfilled in a relationship to keep it healthy. When we are loved and valued, we will feel accepted and our trust will increase for the other person. A healthy relationship is not always about peace, it is also about supporting each other on an emotional level no matter how bad it is. For instance, if you see your partner always smiling and refusing to tell their issues, it means that you need to push them to open up so that you may help and support them. This way, even if you cannot assist them physically, you can help them emotionally.

No matter what kind of relationship we have, we need to respect the other person's time and space. I know that spending time together is important for a relationship to grow. However, we should not become too clingy. We need to let the other person have their own privacy. When they need time away from us, we must let them take their space. We can use this chance to grow as people and to be better in the relationship. We may reflect on the wrong things we do and fix them. We should not get offended when they refuse to spend time with us, perhaps they just need some time alone since we all need it anyway.

Ways to Achieve Conflict Resolution

I have explained that it is normal to have conflicts in a relationship sometimes. We have different personalities from the start and it is impossible to agree on everything. We should not avoid getting into conflicts, but learn how to resolve them so that we can move forward. We have no idea how to manage conflict, our relationship will suffer and might also fail. A conflict needs to be dealt with in healthy and positive ways so that we can bond at the end of it. By doing this, we will establish a relationship that is healthier and stronger.

Before learning how to resolve conflict, it is important to know that when a conflict is left unresolved, it will grow bigger. This means that we must try to address it as fast as we can. In a conflict, it might be difficult to understand other people's perspectives when we are driven by emotions. This is why we have to try to be objective and set our feelings aside to resolve an issue. Because conflicts may trigger strong emotions, we may have a tendency to lash out. If we feel this way, we need to take a step back before resolving the problem. Conflict is not just about problems, but it may also help us establish better connections. We can learn new things from a conflict and apply it to the relationship.

In a conflict, both sides will think that they are in the right and should be the winner. This is why we need to reach an agreement and discover common ground. This is the time when we have to join hands and collaborate against the issue instead of each other. We should find a solution that everyone can agree on so that no one will have a hard feeling afterward. Working together means that we will set aside our differences and search for our similarities. We need to let go of our pride so that we can work out a solution faster with collaboration.

Oftentimes, we want to let go and express all of our emotions during a conflict. However, this is not a good idea because it is not only about us. There is another side that we need to pay attention to. Expressing our true emotions in a conflict might have consequences; this is why we have to learn to suppress them. Before discussing a sensitive issue, we need to calm ourselves first. We have to stay level-headed to find a solution. We should take time to let the negative feelings pass and reflect to find clarity on the issue. It is important to put ourselves together so that we can control our emotions.

We must avoid pointing fingers and blaming others in a conflict. This will actually make the problem worse than before. We have to build a safe environment where the other party can feel comfortable about resolving the conflict. We should also avoid getting defensive because it will make it difficult to talk. We need to open our minds and let everyone explain their side. Let them pour out their thoughts so that everything can be processed properly. When we blame others, no one will trust us anymore because they are scared of getting blamed whenever an issue arises.

The Role of Vulnerability in Building Healthy Relationships

Many of us are afraid to open up and be vulnerable to others to avoid getting hurt. I understand that being vulnerable comes with a lot of risks. However, it can also help us grow our relationships to be more healthy and strong. We do not want to get judged or invalidated when we open up our feelings. We may be scared that our past experiences, insecurities, and fears might drive other people away. Being vulnerable means that we let someone else be our true selves and hand out our hearts to them. In a relationship, it is important to get to know each other, but we cannot do it without being vulnerable.

By being vulnerable, we can establish trust and intimacy with our loved ones. This way, we will also trust the other person that we trust and appreciate their effort for being there for us. We will also get to know each other more easily because there are no secrets being hidden. Being vulnerable shows that we are able to express our thoughts, our values, and our aspirations in life. The other person gets to know our true selves so that we can have a deeper level of connection and understanding.

I realize that being vulnerable is uncomfortable most of the time. However, as time goes on, we will get comfortable after practicing it. For instance, you used to have a hard time telling people about your insecurities and past traumas, but when you start opening up with your best friend, it will be easier to tell them about other things. This means that we are educating ourselves on how to manage and control our emotions and we would not feel ashamed or humiliated anymore about our insecurities. This will show us that we deserve to be heard and accepted no matter what we experienced or felt.

Vulnerability also opens up transparent and honest communication with our loved ones. This means that we can get closer to the other person with better trust as well. Being vulnerable directs us to take accountability for our feelings instead of avoiding issues and blaming others for no reason. This also means we can prevent arguments from escalating or worse. When someone hurts us, we need to respond by being vulnerable rather than lashing out so that they can see how bad it impacts us and our emotions. They will also respond more calmly instead of being defensive to defend their actions or words.

Being vulnerable in front of someone else will make them empathize more with us. Vulnerability makes us show others about our secrets and insecurities that we have probably never told anyone before; it lets the other person see things from our perspective. This will also make them understand our emotions and past traumas. When others can put themselves in our shoes, they can show more empathy toward us and our experiences.

Cultivating Mutual Respect in a Relationship

To grow a relationship, we need to also create mutual respect for each other. This means that we have trust and admiration for our loved ones. This also shows that we have strong positive feelings that turn into respect for them. Respect can manifest in various ways, such as when we can talk about it in front of other people or even in secret when we know how to control our minds.

When we respect someone, we will be open and honest with them. We will let them know about our true emotions and thoughts. When we are dishonest, no one will trust us. Honesty actually enhances respect for each other and makes our relationship last longer. We will feel more comfortable being in the relationship because there is no secret that may ruin it.

Respect will also create stability. Every relationship will go through difficult times and we cannot escape them. People may change and situations can shift without us knowing. Respect helps us make the relationship more stable because tough times will only look like bumps on the road. When we have a good car, it is easy to go over the bumps. When we are mutually respectful, we can stay together for longer and keep a happy and healthy connection.

We have seen how important it is to have mutual respect in our relationship. But how do we develop it? Are you interested in learning this to better your relationship?

The following are some tips to consider:

- **Choosing our words properly:** When we want to establish mutual respect, it is important to watch out for what we say. A rude or unkind comment can destroy mutual respect in the relationship. Words are very powerful because they can hurt people and create conflicts that we cannot go back to. In an argument, it is essential to avoid belittling or ridiculing the other person. We must communicate respectfully and take a step if we are about to use negative words that may hurt others.

- **Giving validation:** When we feel stressed and overwhelmed, we want someone to validate our feelings. We can do the same in our relationship. When the other person is feeling anxious, stressed, or concerned, we need to tell them that it is alright to feel that way. We need to validate their experiences and allow them to feel the way they do.

- **Showing patience:** When the other person makes mistakes, we need to avoid getting angry. We need to be patient and regulate our emotions rather than lashing out. When we show patience, we will make our loved ones feel respected as we work to resolve the issues we are facing. We should learn how to be more patient so that our relationship can flourish through mutual respect.

- **Respecting ourselves:** Before we can respect others, we need to respect ourselves first. By doing this, we can avoid toxic behaviors, such as belittling or mocking other people. We must know our needs and have a good amount of self-respect so that we can respect others.

- **Being attentive:** In order to build respect, we need to give the other person some attention. We need to make them happy and comfortable by showing them that we care about what they want and need. When they come to us, we need to also support them so that they can feel safe being around us.

Creating and Communicating Healthy Boundaries

We can think of boundaries as walls that separate us from each other. We might think they are bad, but why would you want to be separated when building a healthy relationship? The truth is that we can use them to create a balance in our relationship. They are essential to keep us sane and help us to maintain our well-being.

No matter what kind of relationship we are in, it is important to set up our own boundaries and communicate them with the other person. We can begin by observing how we feel and respond to the circumstances around us. What causes us to feel uneasy? What matters to us? What would we prefer to remain private? Perhaps we can even put them into writing so that we can see the patterns to set healthy boundaries.

After knowing what boundaries we want to set, we need to know how to communicate them clearly. In a healthy relationship, everyone has to respect each other's boundaries when they are already set. If someone crosses the boundaries unintentionally, they must know how to apologize for the mistake. When the other person communicates their boundaries but we still do not understand them clearly, we should ask them for more explanation as we go along. If we are not willing to communicate and set boundaries in fear that the other person might retaliate, this means that the relationship is toxic or unhealthy.

Boundaries are not a set thing because we can make adjustments as time goes on. As we become more comfortable with the relationship, it is normal to change our boundaries. Perhaps something that we used to be comfortable with becomes uncomfortable because of our life experiences. We have the right to shift our boundaries according to what we feel at a certain time. As long as we know how to communicate the changes, we will be fine.

Healthy boundaries are made to make us feel safe and protected. They should not become tools to control or harm the other person. For instance, your partner asks you not to talk to other men or women because you might cheat on them. This means that they are being toxic because they try to isolate you from other people. Let's see what healthy boundaries look like:

- **Emotional:** These boundaries make sure that other people respect our psychological and emotional comfort. When communicating an emotional boundary, we can say, "I don't wish to talk about this sensitive topic at the moment because I need to finish my work." This means that we are shielding ourselves from getting too emotional for listening to the other person's issues and emotions. We are not responsible for other people's feelings, so we need to set boundaries to avoid being triggered.

- **Physical:** These boundaries will help us become comfortable when we have to interact with others. For instance, you can tell your parents not to enter your bedroom when you are not there because you deserve privacy. Perhaps you may tell your coworker at work not to put their things on your desk because you like to keep them organized. Maybe you can tell people that you do not like hugs and are only comfortable with handshakes.

- **Material:** These boundaries may involve clothing, money, vehicle, and other material things. If we do not set boundaries for them, people might take advantage of us. Perhaps someone tries to borrow money; you need to say no if you are not willing to do so even if you have enough money. We do not have to give others what we have just because they need it. We have to learn how to say no and protect our possessions.

- **Time:** We have the right to plan our time with what we want to do and this is why we must set time boundaries. If someone asks us to do something for us when we are working, we need to refuse because it might hinder our productivity. Perhaps you can ask your coworker to not call during the weekend because it is the time for family.

- **Sexual:** In a romantic relationship, it is important to set sexual boundaries. This means that we must communicate to our partners that we require consent before we become intimate. This also involves asking our partners if they are comfortable during the sexual encounter. Perhaps you can tell your partner that you are uncomfortable when they do not wear protection, so you prefer to always use it when being intimate.

Practicing Forgiveness and Compassion

We are all humans who can make mistakes and most of us will regret and feel guilty for our faults. This means that all of us deserve to be forgiven. If someone makes a mistake, we have to also forgive them so that we can move forward with the relationship. If we refuse to forgive, we will hold grudges and become bitter toward the other person. This will cause us pain and suffering if we still decide to be in the relationship. Forgiveness teaches us to let go so that we can bond better with others. This will also improve our communication and educate us more about empathy. Without forgiveness, our relationship will suffer and eventually fail because of the resentment that has built up throughout time.

How do we practice forgiveness? Just like anything worthwhile in life, forgiveness involves mindfulness. This means that we need to stop being egotistical and let go of our anger. We need to open our hearts to hear the other side so that we can develop as people. There will be no healthy communication if we refuse to learn how to forgive and forget when the other person makes a mistake.

We need to also look at the times when we make mistakes. When you made the mistake, did you ask for forgiveness? Were you forgiven by the other person? If so, how did it make you feel? Were you happy? Were you willing to change your way after being forgiven? Because we have been forgiven by others, we need to also practice how to forgive other people. I know that it is not always easy to forgive, but we can always try to let go because others have done the same to us.

Rather than pointing fingers and blaming another person, we need to say our truths. We must try to recognize the situations or actions that hurt our emotions. Sometimes the other person might not know what we are angry about. We need to explain the source of pain and be truthful with ourselves and them. When they understand what they did wrong, they may apologize sincerely so that we can forgive easily.

We should not suppress our feelings. In order to move forward, we need to feel and then let go of all the negative emotions. When someone makes a mistake, we will feel anger, frustration, and resentment. We might also feel fear, shock, and shame. We must allow ourselves to feel them so that they do not explode at appropriate times. When we do not process emotions, we can never forgive. By letting go, we can show forgiveness and heal from the pain.

We have to also show empathy toward the other person. Displaying empathy does not mean that they excuse their bad actions or behaviors. This means that we are trying to understand what they feel and think. This does mean that we must agree with their perspectives, but to better understand why they do what they did. Forgiveness becomes easy when we can empathize with the other person because we will listen to them better.

Furthermore, it is important to stay patient. We all need time to forgive because we need to process the situation first. It will take time to learn not to suppress our feelings. Perhaps we might want to force ourselves to forgive, but it is impossible if we have not let go. We need to be kind to ourselves and take a step back to process everything before we can even give forgiveness. We should communicate this with the other person so that they can give us some space.

Navigating Changes in Relationships Over Time

As time passes by, a relationship will change and grow. After years of a relationship, it is impossible to not go through the ups and downs of life. Dealing with the changes is probably one of the most difficult challenges that we have to experience. Even though changes are natural things, some people might be confused about what to do or how they should respond. These changes can make us frustrated or angry, which means that it will be much harder to overcome. This is why we need to understand how to navigate the changes so that we may work together to get through it.

Why do these changes happen? Human beings evolve based on their life experiences. The causes of these changes can be negative or positive experiences. When we see changes happen, we need to look at the roots. Perhaps the other person is having stressful tasks at work, financial issues, family problems, mental health issues, or conflicts with their friends. Positive experiences may also cause changes, such as getting a new position that requires us to move to a new city or country. In order to deal with the changes, we need to understand what causes them so that we can respond accordingly:

- **We must make communication a top priority.** It has been explained before that the foundation of a relationship is having healthy and open communication. In a relationship, we will face life challenges together and must also overcome them with each other's help. This involves knowing how to communicate honestly and openly. I understand as time goes on, we will get comfortable with each other and we assume that we know what the other person's feelings and thoughts are without having to ask them. However, this is not a good idea because we cannot read people's minds and we need to ask them. We should try to speak up and listen to them and work on changes together.

- **We should make time for the relationship.** As we get comfortable with each other, we probably do not think that we should spend time together as much. However, when life changes, the relationship will also change. For example, in a marriage, your relationship after you get immersed in work and kids. When you are busy and have no time for your partner, you might think that they will feel and stay the same. However, your partner may feel ignored or neglected. This is why you need to set aside time regularly to go on dates with them so that you may catch up with the things that happen in your life. This will show that you care about them and the relationship and that your feelings have not changed.

Chapter 8: Personal Growth

Strategies for Enhancing Personal Growth

Personal growth is a journey that we must go through and it takes a long time to achieve. When we intentionally try to develop ourselves and our skills, we will become more successful and satisfied with life. Personal growth also makes us wiser and builds our character so that we become better people. Our growth happens when we make a decision to improve ourselves. Its purpose is to improve our actions, behaviors, attitudes, and situations. Personal growth is also essential if we wish to accomplish different things in life, such as healthy relationships with others, career advancement, financial success, happiness and life fulfillment, healthy minds and bodies, and more.

The following are some personal growth strategies you can do:

- Learning how to manage our temperament.
- Developing the ability to resist the temptation of procrastination.
- Giving our bodies what they need, such as working out and eating healthy meals whenever we have the chance.
- Cultivating a more mindful attitude toward others.
- Increasing our sense of responsibility.

- Shifting our mindsets.
- Developing a more optimistic outlook.
- Learning how to be more productive.
- Trying not to be lazy.
- Improving our skills and knowledge.

Are you interested in growing and developing yourself? If so, you need to learn how to do it appropriately so that you can get the most out of it. Let's explore some tips to consider for your own personal growth:

Pushing Yourself to Keep Learning

The capacity and willingness to learn are strong traits that can improve many aspects of our lives, whether personally or professionally. We can learn in different ways, such as reading, writing, or studying. Another important learning method is to listen so that we can take on the knowledge being passed onto us. When we keep learning, we will grow better every single day because we are not stuck on outdated knowledge or information.

I understand that to get the best education, we need financial stability. Some people are rich enough to get a luxury education that normal people cannot get. However, it does not mean we should give up learning if we do not have the means. Learning can be done everywhere. Through the invention of the internet, information can be accessed easily nowadays. Even if we do not have the internet, we still can go to a public library to read any books we want. There is no excuse to stop learning.

Listening is also an essential part of learning. By listening to others, we can expand our horizons to places we have never thought of before. Perhaps we can watch YouTube videos while cleaning our house. This way, we can achieve two things simultaneously. We can gain new knowledge anywhere and anytime, so it is our time to put in the effort for our personal growth.

Traveling to New Places

Traveling is also an activity we can do to gain perspective in life. If we never visit new places, we will never know that there are people who lead completely different lives than us. By traveling, we can look at new cultures and try to immerse ourselves in them so that we understand how others live their lives. We will also improve our senses and thought processes. Perhaps we may even find positive things others do that we have never thought of before and apply them in our daily lives. We will be challenged to open our minds and hearts to accept new things.

Traveling does not only mean that we have to visit another country. Maybe we can just go to a different city or town to spark our happiness and creativity. When we go back home, we will feel refreshed because of the new experiences.

Volunteering Your Time

Volunteering is a great opportunity to help others, develop new abilities, and acquire insightful perspectives. By doing this, we will also learn how to care and have compassion for those in need. When we help others, we will improve our empathy while also developing our personal growth. We are contributing good things to the community, which will provide us with a sense of achievement. We focus on what we can do for others so that the community grows better. Perhaps we can also find meaning and identity when volunteering because we get to meet new and interesting people.

Before we start volunteering, we need to define what kind of volunteering we wish to do. Maybe we want to volunteer in our local communities or even abroad so that we can experience new cultures. After that, we focus on looking at organizations that accept volunteers like public libraries, international NGOs, community centers, etc. Finally, we need to prepare our application and explain the reasons behind it. Once we get accepted, we need to just enjoy the experience and help as much as we can.

Putting Your Health First

Personal growth means that we have to be disciplined and committed to the journey. This involves giving priority to doing the things that are good for us instead of only doing easy things. This is why we need to care for our bodies and treat them with respect. These days, there are so many temptations to not care for our bodies, such as sugary drinks, high-calorie foods, and processed foods. We might be too lazy to get up and cook homemade food for ourselves so we decide to indulge ourselves in things that are very unhealthy.

Personal life is a journey that takes a long time, which means that we need a healthy body to go through it. This means that we should try to exercise and eat better meals to prioritize our health. We need to take enough vitamins and minerals as well as get proper sleep every night. The benefits do not only stop at having healthy bodies, but our mental well-being will also improve. We will feel better in our bodies to continue to develop ourselves.

Being Creative

By being creative, we can express ourselves while also connecting with our authentic selves and the people around us. Creativity can be done in different ways, such as music, painting, dancing, and so forth. People choose what kind of art they like and get creative with their minds. When we create something, we will share something meaningful to the world. Our arts are a part of ourselves and we put our minds and hearts into making them. Creativity gives us a chance to explore deep within ourselves and makes us more self-aware. We also will learn how to solve problems and overcome challenges that we face.

Creativity is important for personal growth because we will feel more positive when we can create something good and it gives us a sense of accomplishment. This self-expression journey allows us to learn our shortcomings and strengths as well as gain new perspectives in life. When we can do this, we will establish a better future for ourselves.

Managing Your Time

Nowadays, it is very easy to waste our time doing unnecessary things. We might think that we do not have enough in a day, but this is really only a feeling. We all have the same 24 hours a day, but we may be confused about how someone our age can achieve so much. What we need to do is change how we use our time. When we have free time, we must make personal development a top priority so that we can achieve more success. I know that it will be difficult to start, but we must start by getting off the couch and begin taking action.

How do you start managing your time? Let's say you are commuting to work. Instead of surfing the internet aimlessly, you can use the time to read new books, write in your journal, or meditate. As another example, rather than always using your weekend to drink or going out at the club. You can set it to go to public libraries or even volunteer at a local food bank, homeless shelter, or church. The last example is that you can set a limit on how long you will phone each other. Perhaps only 3 to 4 hours a day for entertainment.

Analyzing Your Life

We need to be self-aware to achieve personal growth. This is why we must set aside time to do a thorough assessment of our lives. In order to effectively assess our lives, we need to ask ourselves the following:

- How is your life going at the moment?

- What aspects of your life do you find satisfying? What parts do you think need to be improved?

- What kind of life do you want to live in the next 10 or 15 years?

- Why do you need to develop your life? How do you plan to achieve your dream life?

- What skills or knowledge do you need to advance yourself?

- How long do you require to accomplish this dream life? And what actions must you take? You can make a list of things you must do, set small goals to achieve, and measure your development.

By analyzing our lives, we will also find our weaknesses and then figure out how to better them. Self-awareness gives us the opportunity to plan our personal growth journey. However, it is important to start with baby steps so that we do not get overwhelmed. Making personal change and development takes so much effort and time. We must start as soon as we can.

Putting Yourself Out There

If we wish to be better at communicating with others, we need to put ourselves out there more. We have to realize that if we always stay cooped up in our homes and refuse to socialize, our lives won't be as fulfilling. Perhaps you are an introvert or have social anxiety and feel uncomfortable interacting with strangers.

However, if you refuse to try and put yourself out there, you will never be good at communicating or socializing with your fellow humans. The following are tips to consider if you wish to socialize more. You do not have to follow all of them; only consider the ones that you feel comfortable with:

- **Start up conversations with strangers:** If we want to make new friends and connections, we have to learn how to do small talk. This means that when we are in public places, we can try to chat with someone new. For instance, if you are traveling in a new city and taking the bus. As a conversation starter, you may ask someone sitting close to you about the best tourist destinations to visit. This way, they may even offer to take you around the city. The first time doing this won't be easy, but with practice, we will get used to it. In the long term, our confidence in social situations will also improve because we have learned how to approach strangers and build connections with them.

- **Put yourself in social situations:** I understand that some of us are shy and anxious when we have to face other people and prefer to avoid social interactions at all costs. However, this will not benefit our social lives in any way. If we are scared of social situations, we need to challenge ourselves and practice socializing more. For example, if you usually hide your face when paying for your groceries at the cashier, you can start with a small step by showing your face and smiling. As you practice, you may even try to ask how the cashier is doing and chat about the weather or current news. It can be very scary at first, but as you get out of your comfort zone, things will become easier.

- **Know that no one expects you to be perfect:** When we are in social situations, we might think that we have to always be perfect. This then makes us put on a mask or a facade like we are a performer on stage. The truth is that we do not always have to be funny or smart when interacting with people. We need to be ourselves so that we can appear more relaxed and friendly. We should talk to people casually without forcing ourselves to smile all the time. We must not try to always impress everyone because it will drain our time and energy in the process. Being ourselves means that we will come out less desperate and more interesting to talk to.

- **Get involved in social events:** If we want to take a big step to put ourselves out there, we can try to find new hobbies or interests. Perhaps we can even try volunteering at NGOs or local charities. By doing this, it will be easier to meet others who share our passions and interests. This is an important step to talk about if we have just moved to a new place where we do not know anyone yet. Building connections in our communities will give us a sense of belonging so that we do not get lost in a new place.

- **Accept invitations more often:** When we get invited to an event but decline it, the other person might feel offended and decide not to invite us again in the future. This is why we must accept more invitations even if we are not very interested in the event. By doing this, we can socialize more and also create new connections with new people. Whenever an opportunity to interact with others and boost our communication skills appears, we must use it to our advantage.

- **Compliment others as much as you can:** People will like us if we are being positive toward them. When we meet someone, we need to be kind. If we see someone has a new haircut, we can let them know that it looks good. Our words might have a big impact and make their day. By doing this, they will feel positive about starting a conversation with us. However, we should always show that we are sincere with our compliments so that others can feel the positive effects. There are many things we can compliment on a person, such as their performance at work, new outfits, personalities, or even how nice their families are.

- **Host dinners or brunches regularly at your house:** If we are still scared of meeting new people, we can instead hold events at our place. We may invite our friends, coworkers, and family members to get-togethers. This way, we can spend quality time with those closest to us. We do not have to invite too many people, maybe 2 or 3 people is enough as long as we are comfortable with them. This can create a supportive and happy environment where we can talk and laugh together while enjoying some drinks and meals.

If we are not comfortable meeting many people at once, we can call up someone and make a one-on-one date or meeting. Perhaps we can ask one of our friends to join us for lunch or dinner at a restaurant on the weekend. We may even ask them to come to our home and cook homemade meals for them. We do not need to make a list of activities to do, but we should focus on enjoying each other's company. For instance, maybe we miss our best friends or family members, and we need to tell them that we want to spend more quality time with them by arranging a coffee date.

Prioritizing Self-Care

When learning how to be better at effective communication, we should not only focus on what others want but also on what we need. This is why we must prioritize self-care so that we can understand our needs and desires better. Self-care does not always have to be something expensive, but it should be an activity that we do daily. When we do not prioritize self-care, our energy will drain and we may feel burnout at some point. However, when we practice self-care, we can be present and happy if we have to interact with others. We can start filling up our energy by practicing self-care before we put ourselves in front of other people. Let's explore how to prioritize self-care:

- **Saying no when we have to:** We should not always be people-pleasers because this will affect our mental well-being negatively. Imagine being forced to do something we do not enjoy. It is important to say no when we do not wish to do something, it means saving energy and time for better things that we like.

- **Focusing on things that are in our control:** We must think too much about something out of our control. Focusing on something that is not in our control will make us feel overwhelmed, which might lead to failure. We should concentrate on what we can control so that we can improve them. We may write down what we can and cannot control. After that, we must try to let go of things out of our control.

- **Not overcommitting:** During the day, we need to set a couple of things we should complete and stick to them. If someone asks us to do something for them, we need to decline and explain our schedule. If we overcommit, we might not be able to finish things well. We may also risk the quality of our work. We should plan our day and stay on track as best as we can.

- **Staying connected:** We must have a strong support system that we can rely on in times of need. I know that some of us try to be as self-sufficient as possible, but it is essential to have someone that we can ask for help. A support system does not only help us with materialistic things but also emotional support.

- **Practicing gratitude:** When we practice gratitude, we will feel happier and more content with our lives. When our minds are always negative, we can never feel happy, which leads us to close ourselves to others. By being grateful for the smallest in life, we can shift the way we look at the world. We will find that there is hope so that we can be better people.

- **Surrounding ourselves with positive people:** Toxic people will usually affect our lives negatively because we have to listen to them complain all the time. By surrounding ourselves with positive people, we can smile more and become happier. We can observe the people around us and determine the ones that make us feel positive. We should put in the effort to get closer to them rather than toxic individuals.

- **Not comparing ourselves to others:** Nowadays, it is very easy to compare ourselves with people on social media. We might have asked why we are not as pretty or rich as that influencer. However, this is not a good practice because it will affect our mental health negatively. Instead of spending too much time on social media, we should talk to real people with real problems. By doing this, we can learn not to compare ourselves to others because people have their own struggles.

Conclusion

Congratulations, you have finished the book at last. How do you feel about finishing the book? Do you feel a sense of accomplishment? You now have all the tools to be better at effective communication. This book has provided you with all the insights, advice, and suggestions that you may put into practice in your daily life. The key to this is to practice. Without practice, you will never be able to achieve what you want. Are you ready to get up and start taking your first action?

This book has taught you how necessary it is to have social skills because, without them, you can never be good at interacting and communicating with your fellow humans. If you have social discomfort or social anxiety, you have also learned how to overcome them with ease. Remember, you have to always talk positively to yourself to build your confidence. In order to be effective at communication, there are some skills you must learn, such as active listening, assertive communication, the art of persuasion, and writing skills.

Moreover, empathy is also important in communication and relationship building. Without it, you can never relate to or understand other people's feelings. Empathy is a skill that we can all learn. In learning social skills, you need to understand social etiquette and become culturally competent to easily navigate social situations. Furthermore, to build connections effortlessly, you must learn the art of witty banter and become more charismatic. You also have learned how to maintain long-lasting relationships by showing vulnerability, having mutual respect for each other, setting healthy boundaries, and practicing forgiveness. The most important thing is to develop yourself. This means that you have to keep learning, put yourself out there more, and prioritize self-care.

With all these tips, there is nothing that you cannot do. However, your journey to achieve effective communication skills and maintain healthy relationships will always be smooth. There will be obstacles on the way and you should prepare yourself when they arrive. There will also be pain and headaches to face whenever you wish to learn new skills. Take small steps first rather than going big from the start. Even if your progress is slow, you should feel down and keep staying on track to success. It is time to get off the couch and take action.

THANK YOU!

Dear Reader,

Thank you for choosing "Effective Communication and Empathy: Forge Meaningful Connections and Thrive." Your support means the world to me.

I crafted this book with expert insights and practical strategies to help you master the art of communication and empathy. It has provided valuable tools for personal growth and building meaningful relationships.

I kindly ask for your assistance. Your feedback and review on the platform where you purchased the book would be greatly appreciated. By sharing your thoughts, you support independent authors like myself and help others discover the power of effective communication and empathy.

Your review has the potential to inspire others to develop essential social skills and cultivate empathy, creating connections that truly matter. It fuels my passion for writing and guides me in shaping future content that meets your needs.

Thank you for investing in "Effective Communication and Empathy." Let's foster a world where individuals thrive through effective communication, understanding, and compassion.

With heartfelt appreciation,

Richard Garraway

References

Abass, S. (2016, December 20). *3 benefits of effective communication in relationships*. Life Hack. https://www.lifehack.org/509189/3-benefits-effective-communication-relationship

Abraham, M. (2020, October 10). *What is the difference between shyness and social anxiety?* Calm Clinic. https://www.calmclinic.com/social-anxiety/shyness

Allen, R. K. (2012). *How to build positive relationships*. Roger K. Allen. https://www.rogerkallen.com/build-positive-relationships/#:~:text=1.-,Empathy,%2C%20compassion%2C%20acceptance%2C%20love.

Amaresan, S. (2021, November 19). *27 conflict resolution skills to use with your team and your customers*. Hub Spot. https://blog.hubspot.com/service/conflict-resolution-skills

Amber. (2023, February 17). *Social etiquette: Everything you need to know about behaving well*. Shine Sheets. https://www.shinesheets.com/social-etiquette-rules-and-manners/

Are you socially awkward? (2022, September 16). Cutica Health. https://cuticahealth.com/are-you-socially-awkward

Artz, N. (2023, April 30). *Shyness vs. social anxiety: Understanding the difference*. Choosing Therapy. https://www.choosingtherapy.com/social-anxiety-vs-shyness/

Babiedaite, I. (2023, February 22). *The art of self-expression: Why creativity is key to personal growth.* Medium. https://medium.com/illuminations-mirror/the-art-of-self-expression-why-creativity-is-key-to-personal-growth-54583e4239d8

Barot, H. (n.d.). *13 reasons why communication is important in life.* Frantically Speaking. https://franticallyspeaking.com/13-reasons-why-communication-is-important-in-life/

Betz, M. (2022, September 14). *What is self-awareness and why is it important?* Better Up. https://www.betterup.com/blog/what-is-self-awareness

Birt, J. (2023, February 27). *How to use emotional intelligence skills in the workplace.* Indeed. https://www.indeed.com/career-advice/career-development/emotional-intelligence-skills

Blue, A. (2017, November 6). *Poor social skills may be harmful to mental and physical health.* The University of Arizona. https://news.arizona.edu/story/poor-social-skills-may-be-harmful-mental-and-physical-health

Brooks, H. (2017, April 6). *9 signs you might be socially awkward (plus what your friends & colleagues won't tell you).* Medium. https://medium.com/@Hannah_Brooks/9-signs-you-might-be-socially-awkward-plus-what-your-friends-colleagues-wont-tell-you-a54d471a9121

Brotheridge, C. (2020, July 17). *12 powerful ways to help overcome social anxiety.* Psychology Today. https://www.psychologytoday.com/us/blog/calmer-you/202007/12-powerful-ways-help-overcome-social-anxiety?amp

Brown, N. (2017, October 24). *Eight ways to make a positive first impression.* Entrepreneur. https://www.entrepreneur.com/en-ae/growth-strategies/eight-ways-to-make-a-positive-first-impression/303538

Burgess, J. (2023, May 3). *How has technology affected social interaction?* Sogolytics. https://www.sogolytics.com/blog/how-has-technology-affected-social-interaction/

Chui, A. (2022, June 17). *23 things to make a relationship last and healthy.* Life Hack. https://www.lifehack.org/articles/communication/20-things-to-make-a-relationship-last.html

Clarke, J. (2023, March 1). *Cognitive empathy vs. emotional empathy.* Verywell Mind. https://www.verywellmind.com/cognitive-and-emotional-empathy-4582389#:~:text=Cognitive%20empathy%20involves%20knowing%20how,and%20maintain%20connections%20with%20others.

Cohan, W. (2021, August 19). *Barriers to empathy.* Medium. https://wendylcohan.medium.com/barriers-to-compassion-and-empathy-4e57ba8a2358

Communication skills. (2023). Skills You Need. https://skillsyouneed.com/ips/communication-skills.html

Couples counseling series #2: curves ahead? How to navigate change as a couple. (2023). Blue Boat Counseling. https://blueboatcounseling.com/how-to-navigate-change-as-a-couple/

Cuncic, A. (2020, July 22). *Differences between shyness and social anxiety disorder.* Very well Mind. https://www.verywellmind.com/difference-between-shyness-and-social-anxiety-disorder-3024431

Cuncic, A. (2020, November 27). *Negative automatic thoughts and social anxiety.* Verywell Mind. https://www.verywellmind.com/what-are-negative-automatic-thoughts-3024608

Cuncic, A. (2022, November 9). *What is active listening?* Verywell Mind. https://www.verywellmind.com/what-is-active-listening-3024343#:~:text=In%20communication%2C%20active%20listening%20is,home%2C%20or%20in%20social%20situations.

Curtis, N. (n.d.). *Witty banter: What it is & 15 secrets to talk witty & make people laugh.* Love Panky. https://www.lovepanky.com/my-life/work-and-office/witty-banter-master

Drake, K. (2021, July 1). *How to navigate and embrace change in your relationships.* Psych Central. https://psychcentral.com/blog/change-in-relationships-what-to-do-when-your-partner-changes#why-it-happens

Eatough, E. (2023, March 3). *Cognitive empathy: Learn to be a better leader and coworker.* Better Up. https://www.betterup.com/blog/cognitive-empathy?hs_amp=true

8 ways to enhance cross-cultural competence. (2023). Skills You Need. https://www.skillsyouneed.com/rhubarb/cross-cultural-competence.html

Empathy: What it is, why it matters, and how you can improve. (2023). Masters in Communication. https://www.mastersincommunications.org/empathy-what-why-how/

Ferry, K. (2023). *4 emotional intelligence skills for handling crises.* Korn Ferry. https://www.kornferry.com/insights/this-week-in-leadership/emotional-intelligence-skills-coronavirus-leadership

Fisher, M. (2022, March 28). *How to practice forgiveness in your relationships.* Imago Relationships. https://blog.imagorelationshipswork.com/forgiveness-in-your-relationships?hs_amp=true

5 benefits of healthy relationships. (2021, September). Health Beat. https://www.nm.org/healthbeat/healthy-tips/5-benefits-of-healthy-relationships

Fodeman, D. (2020, January 8). *The impact of technology on socialization and communication skills.* Brookwood School. https://libertyclassicalacademy.org/technology-affects-social-skills/

Haeli, H. (2023, February 16). *How to prioritize self-care and your mental health.* Nivati. https://www.nivati.com/blog/how-to-prioritize-self-care-and-your-mental-health

Hailey, L. (2023). *Be an expert at witty banter – how to charm you're your words.* Science of People. https://www.scienceofpeople.com/witty-banter/

Hall, J. (2023, May 16). *15 ways to improve short attention span and stay focused.* Life Hack. https://www.lifehack.org/885119/short-attention-span#:~:text=Short%20attention%20span%20means

%20that,focusing%20on%20tasks%20or%20discussio
ns.

Herndon, J. (2021, June 10). *What to know about exposure therapy for anxiety.* Healthline. https://www.healthline.com/health/anxiety/exposure-therapy-for-anxiety#how-it-works

Herrity, J. (2023, March 10). *10 ways to develop and improve your social skills.* LinkedIn. https://www.indeed.com/career-advice/career-development/developing-social-skills

Herrity, J. (2023, March 17). *What are social skills? Definition and examples.* Indeed. https://www.indeed.com/career-advice/career-development/social-skills#:~:text=Social%20skills%20are%20important%20because,position%2C%20industry%20or%20experience%20level.

Higuera, M. (2023, February 6). *Social anxiety disorder.* Healthline. https://www.healthline.com/health/anxiety/social-phobia

Himelstein, C. (2021, May 6). *Four healthy communication habits for virtual meetings.* Forbes. https://www.forbes.com/sites/forbescommunicationscouncil/2021/05/05/four-healthy-communication-habits-for-virtual-meetings/?sh=4ae64db82201

Hogan, L. (2021, August 25). *How to be more empathetic.* WebMD. https://www.webmd.com/balance/features/how-to-be-more-empathetic

How to use active listening to improve your communication skills. (2021, November 3). Masterclass. https://www.masterclass.com/articles/how-to-use-active-listening-to-improve-your-communication-skills

Kaur, R. (2023, March 17). *What are social skills? Why are social skills important?* Discovery Building Sets. https://discoverybuildingsets.com/blogs/dbs-articles/what-are-social-skills

Keiling, H. (2023, February 3). *9 types of nonverbal communication and how to understand them.* Indeed. https://www.indeed.com/career-advice/career-development/nonverbal-communication-skills#:~:text=Nonverbal%20communication%20is%20 0the%20transfer,conveys%20friendliness%2C%20acce ptance%20and%20openness.

Lamothe, C. (2019, July 15). *10 tips for being more social on your own terms.* Healthline. https://www.healthline.com/health/how-to-be-more-social#pick-up-the-phone

Lauren. (2023, May 22). *Top reasons why volunteering is important for personal development.* World Packers. https://www.worldpackers.com/articles/why-is-volunteering-important

Learning How to Network at Events Effectively (With Tips). (2022, November 3). Indeed. https://ca.indeed.com/career-advice/career-development/how-to-network-at-events

Lim, M. (2016, November 24). *Explainer: what is exposure therapy and how can it treat social anxiety?* The Conversation. https://theconversation.com/amp/explainer-what-is-exposure-therapy-and-how-can-it-treat-social-anxiety-64483

Making yourself a priority: Best self-love practices. (2023). YMCA. https://www.ymcadallas.org/blog/making-yourself-priority-best-self-love-practices

Marie, S. (2022, April 18). *8 ways to build vulnerability in relationships.* Psych Central. https://psychcentral.com/relationships/trust-and-vulnerability-in-relationships#benefits

Marotta, B. (2017, May 23). *Empathy is the ultimate persuasion tool.* Brendon Marotta. https://brendonmarotta.com/1709/empathy-ultimate-persuasion-tool/#:~:text=Empathy%20is%20the%20ultimate%20persuasion%20tool.,know%20where%20they're%20starting.

Martic, K. (2023, January 18). *Top 13 communication barriers and how to tackle them.* Haiilo. https://haiilo.com/blog/communication-barriers/

Matejko, S. (2022, October 11). *Social awkwardness: Signs and how to overcome it.* Psych Central. https://psychcentral.com/health/socially-awkward

McLaren, S. (2020, May 4). *How to become a more empathetic communicator — and why it will make you a better leader.* LinkedIn. https://www.linkedin.com/business/talent/blog/talent-strategy/how-to-lead-with-empathy-and-compassion

Miller, C. C. (n.d.). *How to be more empathetic.* New York Times. https://www.nytimes.com/guides/year-of-living-better/how-to-be-more-empathetic

Morin, A. (2023, February 13). *How to be more confident: 9 tips that work.* Verywell Mind. https://www.verywellmind.com/how-to-boost-your-self-confidence-4163098

Morin, D. (2021, July 30). *How to be more socially confident (without being fake)*. Social Self. https://socialself.com/outgoing-chapter-2/

Morin, D. (2023, April 3). *How to be more social (if you're not a party-person)*. Social Self. https://socialself.com/blog/how-to-be-more-social/

Naz, Z. (2023, April 21). *Effective communication: Definition, 7 steps, examples.* Knowledge Hut. https://www.knowledgehut.com/blog/project-management/effective-communication

Nazar, J. (2013, March 26). *The 21 principles of persuasion.* Forbes. https://www.forbes.com/sites/jasonnazar/2013/03/2 6/the-21-principles-of-persuasion/?sh=1f1bc1fda4c9

Oberhagemann, J. (2020). *Social dynamics.* Realization Systems. https://realization.systems/social-dynamics/

Ong, J. (2023). *The causes of poor social skills.* Jason Ong. https://ongjason.com/the-causes-of-poor-social-skills/

Pantalone, M. (n.d.). *7 ways to communicate effectively in virtual meetings.* Infinite growth. https://infinitegrowth.com.au/7-ways-to-communicate-effectively-in-virtual-meetings/

Patterson, R. (2020, January 23). *10 ways to improve your social skills and be more outgoing.* College Infor Geek. https://collegeinfogeek.com/social-skills/

Peek, S. (2023, February 22). *Want to be a good leader? Step 1: Know thyself.* Business News Daily. https://www.businessnewsdaily.com/6097-self-awareness-in-leadership.html

Ratka, A. (2018). Empathy and the development of affective skills. *American Journal of Pharmaceutical Education, 82*(10).

Raypole, C. (2019, November 19). *The ups and downs of being socially awkward.* Healthline. https://www.healthline.com/health/socially-awkward#signs

Raypole, C. (2020, August 20). *Assertive communication is healthy, not 'bossy' — here's why.* Healthline. https://www.healthline.com/health/assertive-communication#examples

Rehman, A. (n.d.). *Forgiveness in relationships: How to let go of anger & resentment.* Grief Recovery Center. https://www.griefrecoveryhouston.com/forgiveness-in-relationships/

Reid, R. (2020, July 8). *What is charisma?* Pinnacle Well-Being Sevices. https://pinnaclewellbeingservices.com/what-is-charisma/

Reid, S. (2023, March 1). *Setting healthy boundaries in relationships.* Help Guide. https://www.helpguide.org/articles/relationships-communication/setting-healthy-boundaries-in-relationships.htm

Renner, A. (2014, February 13). *10 reasons why being in a relationship makes your life better and healthier.* Life Hack. https://www.lifehack.org/articles/communication/10-reasons-why-being-relationship-makes-your-life-better-and-healthier.html

Respect in a relationship: How to build respect. (2022, November 1). Masterclass. https://www.masterclass.com/articles/respect-in-a-relationship

Richards, L. (2022, March 18). *What is positive self-talk?* Medical News Today. https://www.medicalnewstoday.com/articles/positive-self-talk#what-is-it

Riserbato, R. (2020, September 3). *Cultural competence: What is it and how to develop it at your company.* Hub Spot. https://blog.hubspot.com/marketing/cultural-competence

Robinson, L., Smith, M., & Segal, J. (2023, February 28). *Tips for building a healthy relationship.* Help Guide. https://www.helpguide.org/articles/relationships-communication/relationship-help.htm

Roncero, A. (2021, June 21). *Automatic negative thoughts: how to identify and fix them.* Better Up. https://www.betterup.com/blog/automatic-thoughts

Sander, V. & Watkins, N. (2022, January 7). *What are social skills? (Definition, examples, and importance).* Social Self. https://socialself.com/blog/social-skills-definition/

Sanders, P. (2022, May 24). *Banter and wit: Everything you need to know.* Get the Friends You Want. https://getthefriendsyouwant.com/banter-wit/

Saporito, B. (n.d.). *How great companies give their people what they want.* Inc. https://www.inc.com/magazine/202305/bill-saporito/how-great-companies-give-their-people-what-they-want.html

Segal, J., Robinson, L., & Smith, M. (2023, February 24). *Conflict resolution skills.* Help Guide. https://www.helpguide.org/articles/relationships-communication/conflict-resolution-skills.htm

Self-awareness and effective communication. (2023, February 10). The Self-awareness Guy. https://www.theselfawarenessguy.com/4573/self-awareness-and-effective-communication#:~:text=Self%2Dawareness%20helps%20you%20communicate,helps%20you%20collaborate%20with%20others.

Sethi, B. (2021, August 19). *Unspoken social etiquette rules everyone should aware of.* Firstcry Parenting. https://parenting.firstcry.com/articles/unspoken-social-etiquette-rules-everyone-should-aware-of/

7 most important social skills for family, relationships, and leaders. (2023). High 5 Test. https://high5test.com/social-skills/

7 tips for personal growth. (2023, March 10). Indeed. https://www.indeed.com/career-advice/career-development/tips-for-personal-growth

7 ways to feel more confident and less awkward in social situations. (2023, May 22). Better Help. https://www.betterhelp.com/advice/relations/how-to-feel-confident-in-awkward-social-situations/

Shadinger, D., Katsion, J., Myllykangas, S., & Case, D. (2019). The Impact of a Positive, Self-Talk Statement on Public Speaking Anxiety. *College Teaching, 1*(68), 5-11.

6 barriers to effective communication. (2018, July 18). Drexel University. https://drexel.edu/graduatecollege/professional-development/blog/2018/July/6-barriers-to-effective-communication/

Surbhi, S. (2018, November 19). *Difference between verbal and nonverbal communication.* Key Differences.

https://keydifferences.com/difference-between-verbal-and-non-verbal-communication.html

Swords, C. (2019, June 5). *Why self-awareness is crucial in your communications.* LinkedIn. https://www.linkedin.com/pulse/why-self-awareness-crucial-your-communications-charley-swords/

10 important social skills to have (definition and examples). (2023, March 24). Indeed. https://sg.indeed.com/career-advice/career-development/social-skills

Ten tips for effective virtual communication. (2023). Huthwaite International. https://www.huthwaiteinternational.com/blog/effective-virtual-communication

The difference between verbal and nonverbal communication. (2023). The Social Skills Center. https://socialskillscenter.com/the-difference-between-verbal-and-nonverbal-communication/

The importance of social dynamics & communication skills in the workplace. (2021). Ticvic. https://www.ticvic.com/blog/the-importance-of-social-dynamics-communication-skills-in-the-workplace/

Types of empathy. (2023). Skills You Need. https://www.skillsyouneed.com/ips/empathy-types.html

Understanding social dynamics and communication skills for employment. (2020, August 14). JIS Group. https://www.jisgroup.org/blog/news-details.php?nid=25

Understanding trouble with social skills. (2023). Understood. https://www.understood.org/en/articles/trouble-with-social-skills

Verbal vs. nonverbal communication explained. (2021, December 21). Master Class. https://www.masterclass.com/articles/verbal-vs-nonverbal-communication

Vishen & White, A. (2022, June 23). *What is personal growth and why is it so important?* Mind Valley. https://blog.mindvalley.com/personal-growth/

Waters, S. (2021, December 6). *How to make a good impression: Expert tips and tricks.* Better Up. https://www.betterup.com/blog/how-to-make-a-good-first-impression?hs_amp=true

Waters, S. (2022, November 9). *How to be more persuasive: 6 tips for convincing others.* Better Up. https://www.betterup.com/blog/how-to-be-more-persuasive

Waters. S. (2022, July 6). *Is it possible to learn how to not be shy? 9 ways to overcome it.* Better Up. https://www.betterup.com/blog/how-to-not-be-shy

Watkins, N. (2022, September 23). *How to be more charismatic (and become naturally magnetic).* Social Self. https://socialself.com/blog/be-charismatic/

What are important conflict resolution skills? (2023). Mailchimp. https://mailchimp.com/resources/conflict-resolution-skills/

What are my boundaries? (2023). Love Is Respect. https://www.loveisrespect.org/resources/what-are-my-

boundaries/#:~:text=Some%20examples%20of%20pe
rsonal%20boundaries,multiple%20times%20in%20an
%20hour

What Is Cultural Competence and Why Is It Important? (2023,
February 3). Indeed. https://www.indeed.com/career-
advice/career-development/cultural-competence

What is effective communication? (with benefits and tips). (2023,
February 3). Indeed. https://www.indeed.com/career-
advice/career-development/effective-communication

Written Communication Skills (2023 Guide). (2023, April 21). Wiki
Job.   https://www.wikijob.co.uk/interview-
advice/competencies/written-communication-skills

Young, K. (2023). *Charisma: How to radiate warmth and confidence.*
Hey   Sigmund.
https://www.heysigmund.com/charisma-how-to-
radiate-warmth-and-confidence/

Made in the USA
Las Vegas, NV
30 September 2024

96003247R00090